The Tastes and Tales of Mōʻiliʻili

Proceeds from the sale of this cookbook will go towards
Mōʻiliʻili Community Center's programs of service

COOKBOOK COMMITTEE

Editor

Muriel Miura Kaminaka

Computer Production/
Production Coordinator

Brian Takeshita

Cover Design

Devon Kohara

Art/Illustrator

Paul Konishi

Layout

David Hamil

Senior Center Director

Jill Kitamura

Publicity & Public Relations

Beth Lum

Stories of Moiliili

Glen Grant

Published by Mutual Publishing, LLC
Fifth Printing — September 2005
Sixth Printing — February 2006

The information contained in this book is accurate and complete to the
best of our knowledge. All recipes and recommendations are made
without guarantees. MCC and the Cookbook Committee disclaim all
liability in connection with the use of the information contained within.

Printed in Taiwan

*Dedicated to the settlers and pioneers of Moiliili
and to those who continue to inspire and perpetuate
its legacy.*

The marsh reeds represent Mō'ili'ili Community Center's
past heritage—the Mō'ili'ili area was
once largely marshland.

The rainbow symbolizes multiplicity—Mō'ili'ili
Community Center offers multiple services for a
multiethnic group of people with
many different interests.

The sun signifies unity—it is a common source of
power, energy, change and growth for all.

PREFACE

THE TASTES AND TALES OF MOILIILI is a compilation of interesting recipes submitted by members, volunteers and friends of the Moiliili Community Center. The recipes, tested in the kitchens of the donors and edited by the Cookbook Committee for clarity and editorial uniformity, reflect the diversity and rich heritage of Moiliili and are printed as submitted. You'll find that we have responded to contemporary trends in cooking without compromising our desire to bring you good local food with the Moiliili flair.

We bring to you a treasury of many "old time favorites," updated to meet today's tastes and lifestyle. In addition, some of the tales of Moiliili will be certain to evoke warm memories of a bygone era for many, and for others, a visit into the past.

This book represents the efforts of many reflecting the magic of friendship and the joy of sharing. We trust that you, the reader, will embrace **THE TASTES AND TALES OF MOILIILI** as a personal expression of *aloha* from the people of Moiliili.

Muriel Miura Kaminaka, C.F.C.S.
Editor

TABLE OF CONTENTS

Map of Moiliili

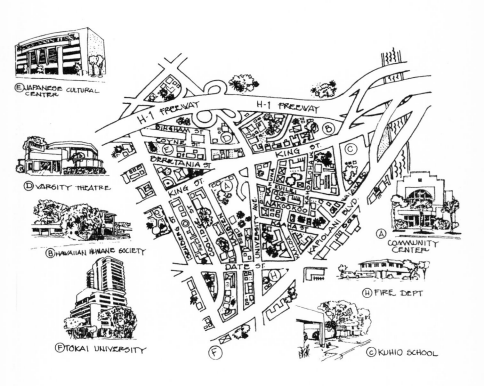

PART I - DISCOVER MOILIILI

How Did Moʻiliʻili Receive Its Name?

One of the most famous legends in ancient times involved the love triangle of Pele, the goddess of the volcano, Hiʻiakaikapolio Pele, her younger sister and Lohiau, the handsome young chief from the island of Kauaʻi.

The story is told how Hiʻiaka, with her friend, Wahineomao, were accompanying Lohiau on a journey back to Hawaii through the district now known as Moʻiliʻili. When they arrived at the place where the old Kamoʻiliʻili Church once stood (now the grounds of the Kuhio Elementary School), a heavy gust of wind blew. Suddenly, Wahineomao and Lohiau felt invisible hands pulling their ears back. Calling out to Hiʻiaka for help, the goddess knew that a moʻo, a supernatural lizard, was attacking her companions. She told Wahineomao and Lohiau to stay near her and suddenly they met the fierce lizard who wanted to fight. Hiʻiaka removed her outside skirt, which held forks of lightning and smote him with it. His body was cut to pieces and the pieces turned into a low hill in the neighborhood of the old Hawaiian Church. Thus, the place was called Kamoʻiliʻili, or the pebble lizard. In time, the name of the area was shortened to simply, Moʻiliʻili.

—Glen Grant

1

FOREWORD
Mo'ili'ili: A Place of the Heart

Historical neighborhoods are often celebrated for the distinctive architecture of their built environment or the important national events which occurred on their streets. These neighborhoods are carefully preserved, frequently visited and always promoted as a "must see" destination for visitors and residents. The "places of history" rightfully attract much of our attention, interest and resources.

Mo'ili'ili is a historical neighborhood of Honolulu that perhaps fails to pass the test of a "place of history." Except for a few of the older commercial buildings along South King Street and South Beretania Street which date back to the pre-World War II era and the plantation-style cottages tucked into streets such as Hausten or Kahuna Lane, the architecture of Mo'ili'ili is neither historic or outstanding. While historic events such as Babe Ruth and Joe DiMaggio hitting home-runs out of the old Honolulu Stadium are nostalgic remembrances, these events were hardly of national significance. The stadium today, in fact, is nothing more than an open park filled with families, children and haunting memories of when this site was Honolulu's sporting center. Mo'ili'ili embraces a rich multicultural legacy that reflects the modern history of Hawai'i, but to the untrained eye, this vibrant cultural heritage is nearly invisible.

In the last few years the residents, businesses and community organizations of Mo'ili'ili have been making a concerted effort to recognize, enhance and share the stories of this distinctive neighborhood. They are doing so not only because they believe this area is a "place of history," but because they recognize it even more importantly as a "place of the heart." Every community acknowledges its unique businesses, special foods or restaurants, neighborhood gathering places or annual collective events that promote a spirit of togetherness. Yet, how many of these vital aspects of a community's identity are often taken for granted until they are lost?

These "places of the heart" of Mo`ili`ili are symbolized in the graceful grounds and ponds of The Willows restaurant, the red-tile decor of Chunky's Drive-In, the aromas of the Mo`ili`ili Mochi store, the lively celebrations in the Kuhio Grill, the sight of ladies in the sewing classes of Kuni's Dry Goods and the precariously leaning, old green structure of the Mo`ili`ili Lawnmower Repair Shop. Today, many of these Mo`ili`ili "places of the heart" have all vanished, left only as memories to those who had the privilege to share in their sights, sounds, smells and flavors. Yet many unique and special places still remain in this truly multicultural neighborhood, from the annual sounds of the Hongwanji Obon festival at the Mo`ili`ili Community Center, to the savory foods of international origin to be found in every nook and cranny, the sweet smells of the numerous flower shops and the laughter of the new generation of Mo`ili`ili children, forming their own "places of the heart."

Once a year, the residents of this district will invite the public to Discover Mo`ili`ili, to recall its ethnically diverse past, to enjoy its ancient and modern legends, to sample its vast array of fine foods and to enjoy the company of its open-hearted neighbors. To celebrate "the places of the heart" is to recognize the deep values which makes Hawai'i a truly unique island home - a home where the peoples of all continents have found a way to bridge differences with commonalities in a spirit of *aloha*.

Glen Grant, Chicken Skin/Honolulu TimeWalks Mo`ili`ili

THE SPIRIT OF MOILIILI

REMEMBERING OUR PAST...

MOILIILI (originally called Kamoiliili or place of the lizard pebbles), once a marsh-land of ponds, lotus farms, rice fields, stone quarry, small shops and businesses offered a rich heritage at the turn of the century.

Queen Kamamalu and her court enjoyed summers swimming in the Kapaakea Springs. Dirt trails connected wooden frame houses...Burning wood heated the water for the furo... A manapua man carried his wares in baskets from a bamboo pole on his back...Beckoned as the "floral capital of Honolulu" and commercial crossroads for neighboring areas.

A thriving Hawaiian community up to the 1800's, it welcomed Japanese laborers into the neighborhood to work the taro patches, rice fields and rock quarry, where rocks were cut for Iolani Palace and Central Union Church.

The food, customs and religions of homelands prevailed as the town endured change and the common interests of many for their neighborhood became molded into a strong, active and closely knit community.

MOILIILI COMMUNITY CENTER...born of the need to serve people, traces its roots to the founding of a Japanese language school in a private home in the late 1800's and the purchase of the present site in 1928. Founded as a council in 1942, it was formally chartered as an association in 1945 and renamed the Moiliili Community Center in 1965.

Its mission, "enriching our lives and our Moiliili Community" is facilitated by providing a place where people can come together and appreciate everyone's fine, unique contribution in bringing about what is best for the community. Its facilities are in daily use by all generations participating in a variety of programs and activities administered by staff and volunteers.

Moiliili Community Center provides residents of Moiliili and surrounding communities with the following support, services and programs to enhance individual, family and community life:

- **Senior Center Program**-those 60+ years, residing within the areas from Ward Avenue to Hawaii Kai socialize, learn, obtain services and stay active by being involved in the various recreational, health and educational activities at the Center.

- **Children and Families Program**-designed to provide supervised activities that promote emotional growth and social adjustment of young children and teens.

- **Japanese Language Program**-a reflection of Moiliili's cultural history where student enthusiasm for learning is increased by the modified curriculum and teaching methods.

- **Informal Education Program**-includes leisure time activities-i.e. dancing, exercise, cooking, crafts, financial management, flower arrangement, etc.

- **Elder Care Services**-offers home care to those who may need assistance to ensure the quality and dignity of everyday living.

- **The Thrift Shop**-located on the ground floor of the Harry and Jeanette Weinberg Building, it offers great buys in new and used clothing and a variety of goods.

- **Support for Community Groups**-the Center offers the facilities to social and service groups to conduct their meetings and activities which are vital to the strength and vitality of Moiliili.

PRESERVING ITS LEGACY

Notes

PART II - RECIPES

What is the
Legend Behind the
Famous Moʻiliʻili Caverns?

In his collection of tales entitled *Legends of Hono-
lulu*, William Westervelt accredits the creation of
Moʻiliʻili's underground caverns and water systems to
Kamapuaʻa, the famed ancient Hawaiian pig demi-god.

One day, as Kamapuaʻa strolled through the district of
Kamoʻiliʻili, he saw two beautiful women coming from the
stream which flows from Manoa Valley. He called to them, but
when they saw his tattooed body and rough clothing made
from pigskins, they recognized him as Kamapuaʻa and fled.

The demi-god, Kamapuaʻa pursued them, but the women
were also goddesses who possessed miraculous powers. They
both vanished into the earth just as he was ready to place his
hands upon them. Changing himself into the form of a great
pig, he began to root up the stones and soil and break his way
through the thick layer of petrified coral through which they
had disappeared. He first followed the descent of the woman
who had been nearest to him at a site near the old Kamoʻiliʻili
Church near the present day Kuhio Elementary School. Down
he went through the soil, but suddenly a great flood of water
burst upward through the coral almost drowning him. The goddess had stopped his pursuit by turning an underground stream
into the door which he had thrown open.

After this narrow escape, Kamapuaʻa rushed to the place
where he had seen the other beautiful woman disappear. Here
he also rooted deep through earth and coral, and here again
a new spring of living water was uncovered. He could do nothing against the flood, which threatened his life. The goddesses
escaped and the two wells have supplied the people of
Kamoʻiliʻili with water for many generations, bearing the name,
"The Wells, or Fountains, of Kamapuaʻa."

—Glen Grant

Pupus

Beverages

Pupus
&
Beverages

PUPUS

AHI TATAKI

This dish is a hit at family gatherings...really different and delicious!

> **3 strips sashimi-ready Ahi fillets**
> **Salt and white pepper to taste**
> **Dried sweet basil**
> **4 pieces shallots, finely minced**
> **2 Maui onions, sliced**
>
> **Sauce:**
> **10 leaves fresh basil, thinly sliced**
> **1 jar (8 oz.) Italian dressing (the one on sale!)**
> **1 large ripe tomato, skinned and diced into 1/2-inch**
> **pieces**

Season fish strips with salt, pepper and dry basil; cover with minced shallots. Singe all sides of fish in skillet on high heat...watch carefully as not more than 1/8-inch should appear brown on all sides and center should still be cold and red. Remove and slice into pieces, slightly thicker than sashimi slices. Arrange neatly over a bed of Maui onion slices. Combine ingredients for Sauce and pour over fish.

Hari Kojima, TV2 Host
Hari's Kitchen and
Let's Go Fishing

> *Once upon a time, Moiliili was a marsh-land area of pristine water ponds, lotus farms and rice fields —all the way to the Ala Wai Golf Course.*

APPETIZER MEAT BALLS

Serves 15-20

3/4 cup soy sauce
3/4 cup water
2 small cloves garlic, crushed
2 teaspoons ground ginger
3 pounds ground chuck beef

In a large mixing bowl, combine soy sauce, water, garlic, and ginger. Add ground beef and mix well. Form spoonfuls of meat mixture into 1-inch balls. Put balls on cookie sheet or large pan and bake at 375°F. 15 minutes, then turn over to bake a few minutes longer.

CHEESE FONDUE

Serves 4-6

3 eggs
2 cups milk
Dash of salt and pepper to taste
4-6 slices white bread, crusts trimmed
4-6 teaspoons butter or margarine, softened
1/2-3/4 pound sharp cheese, cut in slices

Beat eggs; add milk, salt and pepper. Butter both sides of bread and cut each slice in half. In a glass baking dish, place 4-6 half slices of bread. Add cheese slices, then layer with remaining bread. Pour milk mixture to cover bread and cheese. Let stand 15 minutes. Put glass baking dish in a pan of hot water and bake at 300-325°F. 2 hours or until brown crust forms. Serve immediately.

> *Moiliili was predominantly agricultural in the early days, because it was "flat and dry" after the Ala Wai Canal was built to drain the swampland. Numerous truck farms, including both vegetables and flowers, sprang up as more and more Japanese left the plantations and settled in Moiliili.*

COCKTAIL MEATBALLS
Makes About 50 Meatballs

2 pounds ground beef
1 cup cornflake crumbs
1/3 cup dried parsley
2 eggs
2 tablespoons soy sauce
2 tablespoons minced onions
1/3 cup catsup
1/2 teaspoon garlic powder
1/4 teaspoon pepper

Sauce:
1 can (16 oz.) jellied cranberry sauce
1 tablespoon bottled lemon juice
1 tablespoon brown sugar
1 jar (12 oz.) chili sauce

Mix meatball ingredients together and form into walnut-sized balls. Place in a shallow pan. Combine Sauce ingredients and pour over meatballs. Bake uncovered at 350°F. about 1 hour or until done. Serve with toothpicks in chafing dish.

CORNED BEEF PUPU
Serves 6-8

1 can (12 oz.) corned beef
2 or 3 medium-sized potatoes, coarsely grated
1 egg
Oil for deep frying

Mix together corned beef, potatoes, and egg. Drop by teaspoonfuls in hot oil. Deep fry until golden brown and crispy; drain on absorbent paper. Serve hot.

"Artesian springs and lots of clear, free-flowing water in Moiliili" remain vivid in the minds of old-timers.

CRAB DIP   Makes About 2 1/2 Cups

1 can (10.75 oz.) cream of mushroom soup
1 package (8 oz.) cream cheese, softened
1 cup mayonnaise
1 can (7 oz.) crab meat
1 stalk celery, minced
3 stalks green onion, minced or 1/2 cup minced Maui onion
2-3 tablespoons water
1 package unflavored gelatin

Heat soup and cream cheese in saucepan over medium-low heat until smooth and creamy; remove from heat and allow to cool. Mix in mayonnaise and crab meat; mix in remaining ingredients. Serve warm or cold with crackers or vegetables.

Variation:
Substitute canned shrimp or imitation crab for crab meat.

HOT CRAB SPREAD   Serves 8-10

1 package (8 oz.) cream cheese
1 tablespoon milk
2 teaspoons Worcestershire sauce
1 can (7.5 oz) crab meat, drained
2 tablespoons green onion, chopped
2 tablespoons almonds, toasted and slivered

Combine cream cheese, milk, and Worcestershire sauce. Flake crab meat and add with green onions to cheese mixture. Pour into greased 8-inch pie plate or small shallow baking dish. Top with almonds in large circular pattern, and bake at 350°F. 15 minutes. Serve warm with crackers.

FRIED MANDOO
Makes About 2 1/2 Dozen

1/2 block tofu
2 cups Chinese cabbage (won bok or makina), chopped
1 package (12 oz.) bean sprouts
1/2 pound ground pork
2 stalks green onion, finely minced
1 clove garlic, finely minced
1 1/2 tablespoons sesame oil
1 teaspoon salt
Pepper to taste
1 package (12 oz.) mandoo wrappers
1 quart canola oil for frying

Soy-Vinegar Sauce:
3 tablespoons soy sauce
2 teaspoons sugar
1 teaspoon rice vinegar
1 teaspoon minced green onion

To make mandoo, place tofu in a double thickness cheesecloth and squeeze out excess water. Simmer cabbage in water to half-cover for 10 minutes. Drain and cool. Place cabbage in cheesecloth and squeeze out excess water; chop finely; squeeze again. Combine tofu, cabbage, ground pork, green onion, garlic, sesame oil, salt and pepper; mix well. Place one tablespoon filling in center of mandoo wrapper. Fold in half, moisten edges with water and crimp to seal. Fry in oil heated to 350°F. until golden brown on both sides. Drain on absorbent paper. Serve hot with Soy-Vinegar Sauce.

To make Soy-Vinegar Sauce, combine all ingredients and mix well.

> *Prior to the 1800's, the Hawaiians grew taro in Moiliili, then a sparsely populated swampland, which supported native birds as well as taro.*

KAMABOKO DIP
Makes About 2 1/2 Cups

2 blocks kamaboko
1/3 cup mayonnaise
1/2 cup minced round onion
2 tablespoons sweet pickle relish, drained

Remove kamaboko from wooden blocks; grate. Mix with remaining ingredients and serve with your favorite chips or crackers.

LOMI LOMI SALMON
Serves 12

1/2 pound salted salmon
6 medium tomatoes, diced
1/2 medium onion, minced
Pinch of Hawaiian salt
1 stalk green onion, minced

Rinse salmon several times and soak in water to cover 2-3 hours. Drain; remove bones and skin then shred. Combine with remaining ingredients; mix well and refrigerate untii ready to serve.

NACHO DIP

1 pound ground beef, browned and drained
1 large can chopped green chilis
1-2 tomatoes, diced
1 medium onion, diced
1 bottle (8 oz.) taco sauce
1/2 pound Monterey Jack cheese, grated
1/2 pound cheddar cheese, grated

Layer in order given in 9 x 13-inch pan and bake at 350°F. 30 minutes or until heated throughout. Serve hot with tortilla chips.

DRIED BEEF DIP

Makes About 3 Cups

1 package (8 oz.) cream cheese
1 container (8 oz.) sour cream
1 jar (2 1/2 oz.) dried beef, chopped fine
2 tablespoons milk
2 tablespoons instant minced dry onion
2 tablespoons dried or fresh chopped green chives
1/4 cup chopped nuts (macadamia or almond)

Combine all ingredients except nuts and pour into a shallow pan or baking dish. Sprinkle chopped nuts on top. Bake at 325°F. 15-20 minutes. Remove from oven and serve with crackers.

Randy Chee
Aloha Poi Bowl

ROLLED OYSTERS

Makes About 20 Pieces

2 jars (10 oz. size) fresh oysters
Garlic salt and pepper to taste
1 pound bacon
Wooden picks

Drain oyster thoroughly; pat with paper towels. Season generously with garlic salt and pepper. Cut oysters into halves or thirds, depending on size. Cut bacon slices in half and use to wrap each piece of oyster; secure with wooden pick. Place oyster rolls on rack of broiler pan and broil 4 inches from heating unit until bacon is crisp. Serve immediately.

SHRIMP ON TOAST
Makes About 80 Pieces

2-3 pounds shrimp, cleaned and deveined
1 can (12 oz.) luncheon meat
Chinese parsley
2 eggs, beaten
1 loaf day old bread
Oil for deep frying

Mince shrimp, luncheon meat, and parsley very fine (or use blender or food processor). Add eggs and mix well.
Spread shrimp mixture on bread and fry in hot oil heated to 350°F., shrimp side down, until brown on edges. Turn and continue frying until both sides are brown. Remove from oil and drain on paper towels. Cut each slice of shrimp toast into 4 triangles and serve immediately or keep in 250°F. oven until ready to serve.

Note: Shrimp toast may be made ahead of time and kept frozen. To serve, reheat in 450°F. oven 6-8 minutes.

SPINACH ROLLS
Makes about 6 Dozen Pieces

2 packages (10 oz. each) frozen chopped spinach, thawed
1 cup sour cream
1 cup mayonnaise
1/2 jar (3 oz. size) bacon bits
1 package (1 oz.) ranch style salad dressing mix
1/2 cup finely minced green onions
10 flour tortillas (8-inch size)

Squeeze liquid from spinach. Combine all ingredients except tortillas in medium bowl; stir to mix well and spread evenly over tortillas and roll like jelly roll. Wrap in plastic wrap; chill overnight. Slice each roll into 6 pieces, arranging cut side up, to serve.

SHUMAI (Steamed Dumplings)
Makes About 30

- 1/2 pound ground pork
- 1 teaspoon sugar
- 1 teaspoon soy sauce
- 1 teaspoon grated fresh ginger
- 1/2 teaspoon salt
- 1/2 medium onion, chopped fine
- 2 tablespoons katakuriko
- 1 tablespoon sesame oil
- 30 pieces won ton wrappers
- Oil for deep frying, optional

Mix together ground pork, sugar, soy sauce, ginger and salt. Squeeze chopped onions to get as much water out as possible; add to pork mixture along with katakuriko and sesame oil; mix well. Place one tablespoon of the pork mixture in the center of each piece of won ton wrapper; moisten edges with water and pinch edges together to encase filling. Steam in greased steamer 12-13 minutes. Alternatively, deep fry in hot oil until wrapper is browned; drain on paper towel.

TACO DIP
Makes About 3 Cups

- 1 small container (6 oz.) sour cream
- 1 package taco seasoning
- 1 medium avocado
- 1 teaspoon lemon juice
- 1 can (10.5 oz.) jalapeno dip
- 6 stalks green onion, chopped
- 1 large tomato, diced
- 1 small can chopped black olives
- Shredded Monterey Jack and cheddar cheese

Mix together sour cream and taco seasoning; set aside. In separate bowl, mash avocado and mix with lemon juice; garlic salt may be added to taste. Layer ingredients in a baking dish in the following order: jalapeno dip, sour cream-taco seasoning mixture, avocado mixture, green onions, tomato, olives and cheeses. Chill before serving; serve with tortilla chips.

WIKI WIKI PUPUS

Split leftover biscuits or croissants and top with shredded cheese and chopped green chilies. Bake or broil until cheese melts.

On colorful wooden picks: ham cube with pineapple chunk and cheese cube with dill pickle.

Fill cornucopias of sliced ham, luncheon meat or bologna with potato salad, celery stick or shredded lettuce; fasten with colored wooden pick.

Remembering some of the businesses of yesteryear:

Kuhio Grill	*Mori Bakery*
Moiliili Florist	*Moiliili Store*
Moiliili Flower Shop	*Nakamura Garage*
Kanda Store	*Ace Appliance*
Moiliili Beauty Salon	*Jane's(dress shop)*
Aloha Fashions	*Dolly's Dress Shop*
College Pharmacy	*Seto Barber Shop*
Kanda Store	*Standard Trading*
Custom Mode-Hawaii	*Kamada Store*
Motooka Candy Store	*Sanada Barber*
Moiliili Market	*Kuni Dry Goods*
Michael's Liquor	*Moiliili Mochi*
Hirai Tailor	*Shima's*
Eddie Lam's Service Station	

BEVERAGES

COFFEE TROPICALE

**Cracked ice
1 1/2 cups strong Kona coffee, chilled
1 tablespoon sugar**

Fill blender half-full with cracked ice. Add coffee and sugar; blend on "high" until thick and foamy. Serve in tall, chilled glasses.

KONA COFFEE is known throughout the world for its flavor and rich aroma. The coffee plant found its way to Hawaii in 1825 when Lord Byron brought some of these precious plants from Rio de Janeiro. The plants were introduced to the "Big Island" of Hawaii in 1828 by the Reverend Samuel Ruggles where it began to flourish on the Kona Coast.

FROSTED HAWAIIAN COFFEE

**2 cups strong Kona coffee, chilled
1 cup chilled pineapple juice
1 pint coffee or vanilla ice cream, softened**

Combine all ingredients; beat until smooth and foamy. Pour into tall glasses to serve.

FROSTY SHERBET PUNCH

**3 cans (46 oz. each) orange-grapefruit juice
3 cans (12 oz. each) apricot nectar
3 quarts ginger ale
3 quarts pineapple sherbet**

Combine chilled juices. Add ginger ale and sherbet just before serving.

HOLIDAY PUNCH

Makes 3 Quarts

1 package (3 oz.) strawberry flavored gelatin
1 cup hot water
3 tablespoons sugar
1 cup cold water
1 can (6 oz.) pink lemonade concentrate, diluted
     according to can directions
1 package (10 oz.) frozen sliced strawberries
1 bottle (28 oz.) chilled ginger ale

Dissolve gelatin in hot water. Combine with remaining ingredients in punch bowl over ice. Garnish with mint leaves, if desired.

Muriel Miura Kaminaka

HONOLULU PUNCH

Serves 20

2 cans (46 oz. each) pineapple juice
1 bottle (28 oz.) ginger ale
Dash of grenadine
1 pint pineapple sherbet

Combine pineapple juice with ginger ale; add grenadine to tint to delicate pink. Add sherbet and serve immediately in tall glass garnished with mint sprigs and maraschino cherry.

> *At one time Queen Kamamalu's summer cottages were located on the banks of Kapaakea Springs.*

HOT MOCHA JAVA
Serves 12

> **5 cups hot Kona coffee**
> **5 cups hot cocoa**
> **12 marshmallows**

Combine ingredients and serve hot in mugs garnished with marshmallows.

ICED TEA
Makes About 7 Cups

> **3/4 cup sugar**
> **1/4 cup lemon juice**
> **2 tablespoons unsweetened instant iced tea crystals**
> **6 cups water**
>
> **1 tray ice cubes**

Combine above ingredients and chill. Serve over ice cubes.

MOCHA PUNCH
Makes 5 Quarts

> **1 quart whipping cream**
> **1/2 cup sugar**
> **1 1/2 teaspoons vanilla extract**
> **4 quarts strong Kona coffee, chilled**
> **1/4 cup chocolate syrup**
> **1/4 cup coffee liqueur, optional**
> **1/2 gallon vanilla ice cream**
> **Chocolate shavings for garnish, optional**

Whip cream until soft peaks form; add sugar and vanilla gradually and continue beating until stiff. Combine coffee, chocolate syrup and liqueur. Spoon ice cream into large punch bowl and pour coffee mixture over. Top with whipped cream and garnish with chocolate shavings to serve.

STRAWBERRY SPARKLE PUNCH
Makes About 12 Cups

2 cups frozen strawberries
1 package (3 oz.) strawberry flavored gelatin, dissolved
in 1 cup boiling water
1 can (6 oz.) frozen lemonade
3/4 cup sugar
1 bottle (32 oz.) cranberry juice cocktail
1 bottle (28 oz.) ginger ale

Mix all ingredients together, adding ginger ale last.

WAIOLI PUNCH
Makes About 20 Cups

5 cups fresh guava juice
5 cups fresh passion fruit juice
5 cups pineapple juice
1 cup lemon juice
4 cups sugar
1/2 teaspoon red food color, optional

Combine all ingredients; mix and chill well. Pour into
pitcher or punch bowl with ice.

The Original Waioli Tea Room Restaurant

*The Chinese began to settle in the Moiliili-McCully area
to raise taro and rice in the 1870's. However, many soon
left, attracted by the opportunity and activity of
Honolulu's growing business districts.*

Breads

Rice

Noodles

Breads, Rice
&
Noodles

BREADS

BASIC WAFFLE BATTER
Serves 4-6

 1 3/4 cups flour
 2 teaspoons baking powder
 1/2 teaspoon salt
 1 tablespoon sugar
 3 egg yolks, beaten
 1/4 cup butter, melted
 1 1/2 cups milk
 3 egg whites, beaten until stiff

Mix together flour, baking powder, salt and sugar. In a separate bowl, mix egg yolks, melted butter and milk. Blend flour mixture with egg mixture, but do not over mix. Gently fold in the beaten egg whites. This recipe works best with a Belgian waffle iron. Keep the batter refrigerated between batches while waffles are being baked. Place finished waffles directly on oven rack in 200°F.-250°F. oven while remainder of batter is being baked. Waffles should be served hot and crisp. Serve with strawberries, whipped cream and brown sugar.

BRAN MUFFINS
Makes 1 Dozen

 1 1/2 cups bran flakes
 1 1/4 cups milk
 1/3 cup oil
 1 egg
 1/2 cup brown sugar, packed
 1 1/2 cups flour
 3 teaspoons baking powder

Soak bran flakes in milk for 30 minutes. Add remaining ingredients and mix with wooden spoon. Pour into muffin pan greased with margarine. Bake at 300°F. 20-25 minutes or until done.

BISCUITS

Makes 1 Dozen

**2 cups all purpose flour
4 teaspoons baking powder
1 teaspoon salt
1/3 cup shortening
3/4 cup milk**

Sift together flour, baking powder and salt. Cut in shortening until mixture resembles coarse meal. Add milk and stir with fork until just mixed. Shape into ball and knead gently five to ten times on a lightly floured surface. Roll out to 1/2 inch thickness and cut with a biscuit cutter. Arrange on a cookie sheet and bake at 450°F. 10 to 15 minutes or until golden brown.

CORNBREAD

Serves 24-32

**2 cups biscuit mix
1 cup yellow cornmeal
1 cup sugar
1/2 teaspoon baking soda
3 eggs, slightly beaten
1 cup buttermilk
1/2 cup milk
1 cup butter, melted**

Combine dry ingredients together then add remaining ingredients and mix well. Pour batter into nonstick or lightly greased 9 x 13-inch pan. Bake at 350°F. 45 minutes or until done.

BLUEBERRY MUFFINS

1 1/4 cup unbleached flour
1/2 cup whole wheat flour
1/4 cup sugar
2 teaspoons baking powder
1 large egg, beaten
3/4 cup milk
1/3 cup canola oil
1/4 cup honey
1/2 cup walnuts, chopped in large pieces
3/4 cup fresh or thawed frozen blueberries

In large bowl, stir together unbleached flour, whole wheat flour, sugar, and baking powder. In separate bowl, combine egg, milk, oil, and honey; mix well. Make a well in the center of the flour mixture and add the egg mixture, nuts, and blueberries. Stir until all of flour is moistened (batter should be lumpy). Line muffin pan with paper baking cups and fill 3/4 full with batter. Bake at 400°F. 15-20 minutes or until golden brown.

CINNAMON ROLLS

A delicious breakfast roll—you've got to try it! Using a bread machine, bread baking becomes one of the easiest tasks in the kitchen, yet it produces spectacular results!

1 cup water
2 tablespoons butter or margarine, softened
1 egg
2 cups bread flour
1 1/3 cup whole wheat flour
1/4 cup brown sugar, packed
2 tablespoons powdered milk
1 teaspoon salt
1 tablespoon active dry yeast

Filling:
1/3 cup sugar
2 teaspoons ground cinnamon
3 tablespoons butter or margarine, softened

Glaze:
1 cup powdered sugar
1/2 teaspoon vanilla extract
1-2 tablespoons milk

Place water, butter, egg, bread flour, whole wheat flour, sugar, powdered milk, salt and yeast in bread pan of bread machine in order listed. Select SWEET DOUGH cycle.

While dough is being made, grease 9 x 9 x 2-inch pan; set aside. Mix sugar and cinnamon for Filling; set aside. Combine Glaze ingredients; mix until smooth; set aside.

When SWEET DOUGH cycle is completed and dough is ready, flatten with hands or rolling pin into 18 x 9-inch rectangle on lightly floured surface. Spread with 3 tablespoons butter or margarine and sprinkle with sugar-cinnamon mixture. Roll up tightly, beginning at 9-inch side. Pinch edge of dough into roll to seal. Cut roll into 1-inch slices and place in pan. Cover; let rise in warm place 1-1 1/4 hours or until doubled. Bake at 375°F. 25-30 minutes or until golden brown. Remove from pan and drizzle glaze over warm rolls.

Note: Only bread flour may be used instead of a mixture of bread flour with whole wheat flour.

Muriel Miura Kaminaka

ENGLISH MUFFINS
Makes 1 Dozen

1 package or cake of yeast
1/4 cup lukewarm water
2 tablespoons sugar
1 cup milk, scalded
3 tablespoons shortening
1 egg, beaten
4 cups flour
1 1/2 teaspoons salt
Cornmeal

Dissolve yeast and sugar in lukewarm water. Add scalded milk and shortening. Allow to cool; add egg to mixture. Pour mixture into flour, blending and then kneading until firm and elastic. Remove dough from bowl and grease bowl with butter. Return dough to bowl, turn over to grease top. Cover bowl and allow dough to rise until doubled, about 1 hour. Knead dough again and roll out to about 1/2 inch thickness. Cut with a large cookie cutter or a glass. Place on cookie sheet sprinkled with corn meal. Sprinkle more corn meal on top. Cover and let rise until doubled, about 1 hour. Bake each side on hot griddle.

Note: Great with butter and jam. Also good broiled with cheese.

FLUFFY BANANA BREAD
Makes 1 Loaf

1/2 cup margarine
1 cup sugar
2 eggs
1 teaspoon vanilla extract
1 2/3 cups flour
1 teaspoon baking soda
1/2 teaspoon salt
1 cup mashed bananas
1/2 cup sour cream
1/2 cup chopped nuts

In a large bowl, cream margarine, sugar and vanilla. Add eggs, one at a time, beating well after each addition, until fluffy. Sift dry ingredients together and add alternately with the bananas and sour cream to the butter mixture, small amounts at a time, ending with the dry ingredients. Add nuts, mixing gently. Pour batter into greased loaf pan. Bake at 350°F. 1 hour or until inserted toothpick comes out clean.

KONA INN
BANANA BREAD   **Makes Two 1-Pound Loaves**

2 1/2 cups cake flour
1 teaspoon salt
2 teaspoons baking soda
1 cup butter or margarine
2 cups sugar
3 large eggs
6 ripe bananas, mashed
3/4 cup chopped nuts, optional

Sift together flour, salt and baking soda; set aside. Cream butter and sugar until light and fluffy. Add eggs, one at a time, beating well after each addition. Alternately add dry ingredients and banana to butter-sugar mixture beginning and ending with dry ingredients; mix only until blended. Add nuts if applicable. Pour batter into two lightly greased 1-pound loaf pans which have been lined with wax paper. Bake at 350°F. 60 minutes or until done. Cool. If desired, drizzle with sugar icing or sprinkle with confectioner's sugar.

Babe Ruth is said to have slammed a couple of home runs out of Moiliili Field on one of his trips to Hawaii.

LAVOSH
Makes 18-24

> **3 1/2 cups flour**
> **1/2 teaspoon baking soda**
> **1/2 teaspoon salt**
> **1/4 cup sugar**
> **3 tablespoons sesame seeds**
> **1/4 cup margarine, softened**
> **1/4 cup butter, softened**
> **1 cup buttermilk**

Sift together flour, baking soda and salt; add sugar and sesame seeds. Add softened butter and margarine; knead in. Add buttermilk and mix further. Roll dough into golf ball-sized balls and roll each flat on a cutting board sprinkled with flour. Place flattened dough on ungreased cookie sheet and bake at 350°F. about 7 minutes on bottom oven rack, and 7 additional minutes on top rack. As an alternative, leave baking sheets stationary on one rack and bake 14-20 minutes or until browned and crisp. Two sheets should be baked at a time. Remove from oven and allow to cool. If lavosh is not crispy, bake a few minutes more.

Representative Scott K. Saiki

MANGO BREAD
Makes 1 Loaf

A delicious breakfast or dessert fruit bread from the Ilikai Hotel's former Executive Chef (circa 1974)

> **2 cups all purpose flour**
> **2 teaspoons baking soda**
> **2 teaspoons cinnamon**
> **1/2 teaspoon salt**
> **3 eggs, well beaten**
> **1 1/2 cups sugar (use 1/4 cup less if mangoes are sweet)**

3/4 cup salad oil
2 cups diced mangoes
1/2 cup chopped nuts or raisins, optional

Sift together flour, baking soda, cinnamon and salt; make a well in the center and set aside. Beat together eggs, sugar and oil; pour into center of dry ingredients and mix well, adding mangoes, raisins or nuts last. Pour batter into a greased one-pound loaf pan and bake at 350°F. 1 hour or until done.

ORANGE ROLLS
Make 12-18

3 cups flour
4 1/2 teaspoons baking powder
3/4 teaspoon salt
3 tablespoons sugar
1 egg
3/4 cup milk

Filling:
1/4 cup orange rind, grated fine
1/4 cup butter, softened
3/4 cup sugar

Mix flour, baking powder, salt, sugar, egg and milk together until mixture is biscuit-like. Divide dough in half and roll out on floured surface into rectangles about 1/2-inch thick. Set aside. To prepare Filling, mix orange rind, butter and sugar together and spread mixture on dough. Roll up like a jelly roll; cut into 3/4-inch pieces. Bake at 425°F. 10-12 minutes or until light brown.

> *The Star Super Market is where Kikutaro Matsumoto's Store once stood. He was considered Hawaii's first Japanese Millionaire.*

NAAN BREAD

Makes 8 Pieces

4 cups all purpose flour
1 tablespoon granulated sugar
1 tablespoon baking powder
1/4 tablespoon baking soda
1 1/2 teaspoons salt
2 eggs
1/4 cup plain yogurt
3/4 cup milk
2 tablespoons canola oil

In a deep bowl combine dry ingredients and mix well. Make a well in center and add the remaining ingredients. Mix all ingredients until dough is somewhat sticky; add warm water, if necessary. Knead dough a little on a floured surface until dough is somewhat elastic. Pinch off golf ball size pieces of dough and place on buttered pan to rest. Cover with damp cloth and let rise for about 1 hour. Dough may also be refrigerated for later use at this point. To cook, pat dough balls into thin circles, about 6 inches in diameter (they should look like tortillas when ready); place on sheet pan and bake at 450° F. 2-4 minutes or until dough puffs up and is slightly brown. Serve hot.

Ram Arora, Owner/Chef
India House Restaurant

Note: These rolls burn easily so keep a watchful eye on them while baking.

During the 19th century, King Lunalilo held most of the Kamoiliili-Kapaakea lands.

PINEAPPLE NUT BREAD

Makes 1 Loaf

1 3/4 cups all purpose flour
2 teaspoons baking powder
1/2 teaspoon salt
1/4 teaspoon baking soda
3/4 cup macadamia nuts or walnuts, chopped
3/4 cup brown sugar, packed
3 tablespoons butter or margarine, softened
2 eggs
1 cup crushed pineapple, undrained
2 tablespoons sugar
1/2 teaspoon cinnamon

Sift together flour, baking powder, salt and baking soda. Stir in nuts and set aside. Cream brown sugar, butter and eggs until fluffy. Stir flour mixture into butter and egg mixture, then stir in pineapple. Pour into a greased 9 x 5 x 3-inch loaf dish. Combine sugar and cinnamon and sprinkle over top. Bake at 350°F. 50 to 60 minutes or until done.

By the 1920's, a small, but self-sufficient community - Moiliili - had developed along King Street with flower shops, meat, vegetable and produce markets by the Japanese lining the then dirt road.

Breads, Rice and Noodles

WHOLE WHEAT BREAD
Makes 1 large loaf

There is nothing quite as delicious as fresh, warm, homemade bread baked in the bread machine!

    1 1/3 cups water
    2 tablespoons butter or margarine, softened
    1 1/2 cups bread flour
    2 cups whole wheat flour
    1/4 cup brown sugar, packed
    1 1/2 teaspoons salt
    2 teaspoons active dry yeast

Place water, butter or margarine, bread flour, whole wheat flour, sugar, salt and yeast in bread pan of bread machine in order listed. Set bread machine for WHOLE WHEAT, MEDIUM crust color, LARGE size, START, unless delay bake is desired. Press START and the bread will be done in the number of hours indicated. When the bread is done, invert bread pan to remove bread; brush with butter and let cool 15 minutes before slicing. Enjoy!

Note: Bread flour may be substituted with whole wheat flour to make 100% whole wheat bread. This bread can be baked in a conventional oven at 350°F. 30-35 minutes in two 9 1/2-inch loaf pans.

Muriel Miura Kaminaka

ZUCCHINI BREAD
Makes 2 Loaves

    3 eggs
    2 cups sugar
    1 cup canola oil
    2 cups grated zucchini
    1 tablespoon vanilla extract

36

3 cups flour
1 teaspoon salt
1 teaspoon baking soda
1/4 teaspoon baking powder
1 tablespoon ground cinnamon
1 cup chopped nuts

Beat eggs until light and foamy. Add sugar, oil, zucchini and vanilla. Combine dry ingredients separately in another bowl; stir into zucchini mixture. Add nuts and pour into two greased one-pound loaf pans. Bake at 350°F. 1 hour or until done. Cool.

WHOLE WHEAT PORTUGUESE
SWEET BREAD   Makes 1 Large Loaf or 2 Small Loaves

A new variation to one of our favorite breads. Sweet bread was traditionally served as an Easter bread in Portugal, but is now available year-round in Hawaii...one of my favorite break- fast breads! I let the bread machine do the kneading, then remove it from the machine and let it rise and bake according to the conventional timetable.

1/4 cup milk
1/4 cup warm water
1/4 cup mashed potato (1/4 cup water + 3 tablespoons
        potato flakes)
1/4 cup butter, melted
3 large eggs
1 teaspoon lemon extract
3 cups bread flour
1 cup whole wheat flour
1 cup sugar
1 teaspoon salt
1 tablespoon active dry yeast

Place all ingredients in bread pan of bread maker in the order listed. Select SWEET DOUGH cycle. Grease two 8 1/2 x 4 1/2-inch loaf pans. Remove dough from bread pan. Punch down dough and divide in half. Flatten dough for each loaf with hands or rolling pin into a 18 x 9-inch rect- angle. Fold crosswise into thirds, overlapping the two sides. Flatten or roll into 9-inch square. Roll dough tightly, begin- ning at one of the open (unfolded) ends, to form a loaf.

In the early 1900's many Japanese laborers, who were leaving the plantations following the abolishment of contract labor with annexation, obtained leases to lands that had formerly belonged to Hawaiians who lost them to the large estates.

Press with thumbs to seal after each turn; pinch edge firmly to seal. Press each end with side of hand to seal. Fold ends under loaf and place, seam side down, in pans. Brush loaves with egg wash; cover and let rise in warm place 35-50 minutes or until doubled. Bake at 350°F. 30-35 minutes or until loaves are golden brown and sound hollow when tapped. Remove from pans; brush with melted butter, if desired. Cool on wire rack.

Bread Machine Method: Place all ingredients in bread pan of bread maker in the order listed. Select

bread type: SWEET

crust color: LIGHT

loaf size: LARGE

press: START and bread will be done in the number of hours indicated. Remove from pans; brush with melted butter, if desired. Cool on wire rack.

Muriel Miura Kaminaka

RICE

BIKO

 2 1/2 pounds mochi rice
 1 cup coconut milk
 1/2 cup dark brown sugar, packed
 1/2 cup light brown sugar, packed

Cook mochi rice as you would cook regular rice. In saucepan, combine coconut milk with sugar and cook over low heat until thick. Reserve 1/2 cup and add remainder to the cooked rice. Line a 9 x 13-inch pan with foil; pour in the mixed mochi rice and press evenly. Brush with the reserved 1/2 cup of milk mixture. Bake at 350° F. 20-25 minutes. Cool and cut into squares.

JAMBALAYA

A delicious Cajun type dish that is enjoyed by many — try it, you'll like it!

 1 cup chopped onion
 1 cup chopped green bell pepper
 1 clove garlic, minced
 2 tablespoons canola oil
 2 cans (1 lb. size) whole tomatoes, undrained and
      chopped
 1 can (6 oz.) tomato paste
 1 can (4 oz.) sliced mushrooms, undrained
 1 cup cooked rice
 3/4 teaspoon salt
 1/8 teaspoon ground thyme
 1/8 teaspoon cayenne pepper
 1 bay leaf
 1/2 pound cooked shrimp, peeled and deveined
 3/4 cup chopped fresh parsley

In a large skillet, sauté onion, green pepper and garlic in hot oil. Add tomatoes, tomato paste, mushrooms, rice, seasonings and bay leaf. Cover and bring to a boil. Reduce heat and simmer on low for 30-45 minutes. Remove from heat and let stand 5 minutes. Remove bay leaf; stir in shrimp and parsley just before serving.

Muriel Miura Kaminaka

KOREAN STYLE FRIED RICE   **Serves 6-8**

1/4 pound pork, thinly sliced
1/4 teaspoon sesame seed oil
1/4 teaspoon sugar
1 1/2 tablespoons soy sauce
1 clove garlic, pressed

2 tablespoons canola oil
1 package (12 oz.) bean sprouts, washed and drained
3 cups cold, cooked rice
3 tablespoons soy sauce
1 cup minced green onion

Marinate pork in sesame oil, sugar, soy sauce and garlic for 15 minutes. Stir-fry pork in hot oil for 2-3 minutes or until cooked through. Add bean sprouts and rice; stir-fry additional 2 minutes or until rice is heated through. Add soy sauce and green onion; toss until well mixed. Serve hot.

> *Kapaakea Lane, tucked between towering highrises and neighborhood stores, was the main access from King Street to the homes behind the Moiliili Community Center. At one time, families kept vegetable gardens and raised pigs there ... even sumo wrestling matches were held there.*

PAN SUSHI

Makes 24-30 Pieces

If you love sushi but find it to be a bother to prepare, you've got to try Pan Sushi... it's really simple to make. It's great for family gatherings, potlucks, picnics and tailgating.

12 cups prepared Sushi Rice

Toppings:
2 cans tuna, drained
2 tablespoons mirin
1/4 cup sugar
1/4 cup soy sauce
Red or green oboro (shrimp flakes)
Thin fried egg strips
Beni shoga (pickled red ginger), optional

Stir-fry tuna, mirin, sugar and soy sauce for 1-2 minutes, stirring constantly.

Line 9 x 13-inch pan with waxed paper. Sprinkle shrimp flakes evenly in pan. Sprinkle with egg strips, then with seasoned tuna. Top with Sushi Rice. Cover with waxed paper and press down firmly. Cool. To serve, invert on serving tray; cut into desired pieces. Garnish with beni shoga, if desired.

Muriel Miura Kaminaka

SUSHI RICE

Makes 12 Cups

1/4 cup vinegar
1/2 cup sugar
3 teaspoons salt
1 teaspoon MSG, optional
4 cups rice, cooked

Combine vinegar, sugar, salt and MSG in a saucepan; bring to a boil and cook over medium heat until sugar dissolves. Sprinkle over hot rice; cool immediately and use to make sushi of your choice.

SPANISH RICE

Serves 6-8

A popular school lunch in the fifties and still a favorite with many.

1/2 cup chopped onion
1/2 cup chopped green bell pepper
1 clove garlic, minced
1 tablespoon canola oil
1 can (28 oz.) tomatoes, undrained and chopped
3/4 cup long grain rice
1 teaspoon sugar
1 teaspoon chili powder
1/8 teaspoon pepper
Several dashes bottled hot pepper sauce, optional
1 1/4 cups water
1/2 cup shredded cheddar cheese, optional

Cook onion, green pepper and garlic in hot oil until tender but not brown. Stir in undrained tomatoes, rice, sugar, chili powder, pepper, hot pepper sauce and water. Bring to a boil; reduce heat. Cover and simmer for 20-25 minutes or until rice is cooked and most of the liquid absorbed. Sprinkle with cheese, if desired.

During the days of the Stone Quarry, a low pitched whistle sounded at 4:00 p.m. every work day to signal the blasting of the blue rocks in the quarry. Constant blasting over the years left the area coated with thick, white quarry dust.

SPANISH RICE CON CARNE   Serves 6-8

1 pound ground beef
4 slices bacon, diced
1 cup onion, chopped
1/2 cup bell pepper, chopped
1 can (10.75 oz.) condensed tomato soup
1 can (14 oz.) stewed tomatoes
Pinch each of garlic salt, oregano and basil
1 1/2 cups uncooked rice

Sauté bacon in skillet until crisp and drain excess fat. Add ground beef and brown; drain excess fat. Add onions and bell pepper; cook until tender. Add tomato soup and 1 can water, then stewed tomatoes; add garlic salt, oregano and basil. Wash rice, drain completely and place in a 4-quart casserole dish. Add beef mixture and mix well. Bake, covered, at 350°F. 45-60 minutes, stirring occasionally until almost all of the liquid has been absorbed. Remove cover and bake another 5 minutes.

NOODLES

CHOW FUN   **Serves 6-8**

Remembering that it was always a treat to buy a plateful of chow fun on Saturdays for lunch.

> **2 tablespoons canola oil**
> **1/2 pound char siu, cut into strips**
> **1 small onion, sliced**
> **1 medium carrot, julienned**
> **3 sheets look fun noodles, cut into 1/2-inch strips**
> **2 tablespoons soy sauce**
> **2 tablespoons oyster sauce**
> **1/4 teaspoon pepper**
> **1 package (12 oz.) bean sprouts**
> **1/2 cup green onion, cut into 1-inch lengths**

Heat oil in a large skillet or wok and stir-fry char siu for 15-20 seconds. Add onion slices and carrots; stir-fry 20 seconds. Stir in look fun, soy sauce, oyster sauce and pepper. Add beans sprouts and green onion; stir-fry additional 10 seconds.

The section between Kahoaloha Lane and University Avenue on South King Street has always been considered the Moiliili business area. In the past, the makai side of the street had two bakeries, a tailor shop, a butcher shop, a tofu store and general stores. On the mauka side, hasu (lotus) farms were replaced by a piggery, a sumo wrestling ring and an outdoor theatre.

HIDEO'S EASY GYOZA

Makes 24-36

**1 pound lean ground pork or beef
5-6 cups cabbage, finely chopped
3 cloves fresh garlic, pressed
2 tablespoons grated fresh ginger
1 package (16 oz.) mandoo pi (wrapper)
Salt to taste
Canola oil for frying**

**Dipping Sauce:
1/4 cup soy sauce
1-2 teaspoons sesame or chili oil**

Brown meat in 1 tablespoon oil; add garlic and ginger and continue to cook. When meat is done, add cabbage; salt to taste and cook until cabbage is tender. Remove from heat; cool.

To make gyoza, place about 1 tablespoon meat mixture in center of mandoo wrapper. Moisten outer edge with water then fold over; press edges firmly together to seal. Pan-fry gyoza in hot oil over medium heat until golden brown on both sides. Combine ingredients for Dipping Sauce in a dish; serve with gyoza.

Lue Zimmelman
Nuimono-Hawaii

The first Japanese immigrants, Kihachi and Shika Kashiwabara, settled in Moiliili in January, 1894. A large banyan tree located in the Moiliili Triange Park is dedicated to them.

HIYA SOMEN

Serves 3-4

1 package (8 oz.) somen
8 cups water
3/4 teaspoon salt
1/2 teaspoon sesame or canola oil

Dashi:
3 1/2 cups water
2 packages (0.225 oz. each) dashi-no-moto
1/2 cup soy sauce
2 tablespoons sugar
1 teaspoon salt

Condiments:
Kamaboko strips
Ajitsuke nori
Shiitake, softened in water
Minced green onions

Spread somen in 8 cups of boiling water and add salt. Cook over high heat until water comes to a boil; lower heat and cook 2-3 minutes or until noodles are cooked. Drain in colander and rinse with cold water. Toss with sesame or canola oil; refrigerate.

Bring Dashi ingredients to a boil; simmer 1-2 minutes and cool. Sprinkle condiments over somen and serve with cooled Dashi.

The area on which the Moiliili Community Center now stands was once used as an open theater where movies were shown and "shibais" (live theatre) were enacted.

Breads, Rice and Noodles

INSTANT SPAGHETTI

Serves 4

1 pound ground beef
1 tablespoon oil
1 round onion
1 clove garlic, mashed
1 can (10.75) tomato soup
1 can (8 oz.) tomato sauce
1 can (4 oz.) button mushroom
1/4 teaspoon salt
1 tablespoon sugar
2 tablespoons catsup

1 package (16 oz.) spaghetti, cooked as directed on package

Brown ground beef in skillet. Add all other ingredients except spaghetti and simmer 20 minutes. Serve sauce over cooked spaghetti.

INSTANT YAKI UDON

Serves 4

2 tablespoons salad oil
1 small onion, chopped
1 green pepper, chopped
2 tablespoons green onions, optional
2-3 packages (7 oz. each) Udon
2 packages udon soup base
1 can (4 oz.) Vienna sausage, sliced
1/2 teaspoon MSG, optional

In heavy skillet heat oil and stir fry onion, green pepper and green onion on medium heat until done. Add udon and fry for 5 minutes on low heat. Add udon soup base and stir. Add sausage and MSG; cook for 5 minutes, stirring occasionally.

LASAGNE NO. 1

1/2 cup chopped onion
1 clove garlic, minced
2 tablespoons canola oil
1 pound lean ground beef
2 cans (8 oz. each) tomato sauce
1 cup water
1 teaspoon salt
1/2 teaspoon oregano
1/4 teaspoon pepper
1/2 teaspoon sugar
8 oz. lasagne noodles, cooked and drained
2 cups shredded cheddar cheese
8 oz. sliced mozzarella cheese

Sauté onion and garlic in hot oil. Add meat; brown. Add tomato sauce, water and seasonings; cover and simmer over low heat 20 minutes. Place half of noodles in bottom of 9 x 13-inch baking dish. Spread half of cheddar or American cheese over noodles. Top with half of mozzarella cheese slices and half of the meat sauce. Repeat layers. Bake at 350°F. 30-45 minutes.

NOTE: Cottage cheese and shredded Parmesan cheese may be substituted for cheddar cheese.

Muriel Miura Kaminaka

Kalo Lane, located between Puck's Alley and the Kamada Building on South King St., was once filled with vintage wooden homes. During early evenings, the smell of burning of wood permeated the air as water was being heated for the furo (Japanese style bath).

LASAGNE NO. 2

Serves 6-8

1 pound ground beef
3 cans (6 oz. each) tomato paste
1 can (14.5 oz.) stewed tomatoes
1 tablespoon Italian seasoning
1 clove garlic, crushed or minced
3 cups ricotta cheese
1/2 cup parmesan cheese
1/2 teaspoon salt
2 eggs
2 teaspoons parsley
1 package (8 oz.) Lasagne noodles, cooked and drained
1 package (8 oz.) shredded mozzarella cheese

In medium saucepan, combine ground beef, tomato paste, stewed tomatoes, Italian seasoning and garlic; bring to boil, then reduce heat to low and simmer for 1 hour. In a mixing bowl, combine ricotta and parmesan cheese, salt, eggs, and parsley; mix well. In 12 1/2 x 9 1/2 x 2-inch baking pan, layer cooked lasagne noodles, meat mixture and cheese mixture. Cover with mozzarella cheese and bake at 350°F. 30 minutes.

SAIMIN

Serves 4-6

A favorite snack or light meal for all of us! Prior to the days of instant soup bases and frozen, ready-to-eat saimin, saimin was prepared as follows:

Soup Stock:
9 cups water
1/4 cup dried shrimp
1 piece (6 inches) dashi konbu
2-3 small pork bones
Dash pepper
2 teaspoons soy sauce
1 1/2 teaspoons salt

2 packages (9.5 oz. size) fresh saimin noodles
1/2 cup chopped green onions

1/4 pound char siu, cut into strips
8-12 slices kamaboko

Combine water, shrimp, konbu, bones, pepper, soy sauce and salt in large pot to prepare Soup Stock; bring to a boil over high heat; lower heat and simmer 30 minutes; strain.

Cook noodles according to package directions. Pour into colander; drain and place noodles in soup bowls. Pour hot soup stock over noodles and garnish with green onions, char siu and kamaboko.

Note: Cooked bean sprouts or cabbage may be placed atop the noodles, if desired.

QUICK YAKISOBA
Serves 2 -4

1 cup cooked chicken or char siu, thinly sliced
1 tablespoon sesame oil
1 package (9 oz.) chop suey vegetable mix
1 package (10 oz.) yakisoba noodles
Oyster sauce to taste
Chinese parsley for garnish, optional

Stir-fry meat in hot oil; add vegetables and cook until slightly tender. Add noodles and more oil, if needed. Add oyster sauce to taste. Stir and cook until noodles are heated through. Garnish with Chinese parsley, if desired.

Lue Zimmelman
Nuimono-Hawaii

SKILLET SPAGHETTI

1 pound lean ground beef
2 tablespoons canola oil
1/3 cup minced onion
1/3 cup chopped green bell pepper
1 can (No. 303) tomatoes and juice
1/2 cup catsup
1/2 teaspoon salt
1/4 teaspoon pepper
1 tablespoon Worcestershire sauce
1/2 cup water
6 ounces spaghetti, broken into 1-inch pieces

Brown beef in hot oil in skillet. Add remaining ingredients;
mix well. Cover and simmer over low heat for 45 minutes or
until spaghetti is cooked.

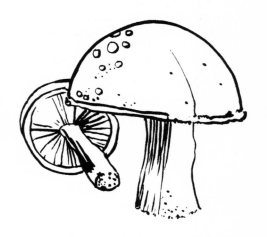

Notes

Meats - Beef

Meats - Pork

Poultry

Main Dishes
Meats, Poultry, Fish & Seafoods

Fish & Seafoods

MEATS - BEEF

BARBECUE BEEF   Serves 4

1 pound stew meat
1 onion, sliced
2 quarts water
1/2 cup catsup
2 teaspoons prepared mustard
1/4 cup brown sugar, packed
2 tablespoons vinegar
2 tablespoons French dressing
Salt and pepper to taste

Cook stew meat and onions in water for 2 hours or until tender. Leave 1 to 1 1/2 cups of liquid with meat after cooking; drain remainder. Shred meat into fine pieces. In another pot, mix catsup, mustard, brown sugar, vinegar, French dressing, salt and pepper; cook 15-20 minutes. Add mixture to meat. Serve over steamed rice or on hamburger buns.

BARBECUED BEEF BRISKET   Serves 8-12

1 4-8 pound beef brisket
1/2 bottle (3.5 oz.) liquid smoke
1 tablespoon garlic salt (more if desired)
1/2 cup Worcestershire sauce
1 cup barbecue sauce

Rub meat with liquid smoke, garlic salt and Worcestershire sauce. Wrap tightly in aluminum foil and marinate overnight. Keeping foil on, bake at 300°F. 3 hours. Open foil and pour barbecue sauce over meat and reseal tightly; bake an additional hour.

BARBECUED SHORTRIBS

5 pounds meaty shortribs, cut in 2-inch pieces
2 medium onions, sliced
2 teaspoons vinegar
2 tablespoons Worcestershire sauce
1 tablespoon salt
1 teaspoon paprika
1 teaspoon chili powder
3/4 cup tomato catsup
1/2 teaspoon cayenne pepper
1/2 teaspoon black pepper, optional
3/4 cup water

Sprinkle shortribs with salt and pepper to taste; dredge in flour. Place in a roaster and cover with onions. Combine remaining ingredients; mix well and pour over shortribs. Cover and bake at 350°F. 3 hours, basting occasionally and turning meat over once or twice during baking. Remove cover during last 15 minutes of baking.

Note: This can be cooked a day or two ahead and refrigerated. Remove and discard solidified grease before reheating to serve.

(Huluhuluwaena, the limu that went so well with raw oio; wawaeiole, the rat's feet limu that almost everyone likes; lipepe that grew amongst the base of the thorny-leafted limu kala; limu eleele that is added to beef stew; manauwea, the "ogo" that the Japanese especially like; and limu kohu when mixed with inamona (roasted kukui nut) and minced nioi (Hawaiian chili pepper) to make "i'a maka" or poke.)

BEEF STROGANOFF

Serves 4

2 pounds sirloin tip, sliced
2 tablespoons butter
1/2 cup chopped onion
2 cups fresh mushrooms, sliced
1 1/2 cups beef bouillon
2 1/2 tablespoons flour
2 tablespoons sherry
1 cup sour cream
1/2 teaspoon salt
Pepper to taste

In large pan, brown meat in butter. Push meat to one side of pan and brown onions and mushrooms. Add broth and bring to a boil. Blend flour with sherry to make paste and stir into pan, cooking until slightly thick. Reduce to low heat and add sour cream. Add salt and pepper; serve over egg noodles.

EASY BEEF STROGANOFF

Serves 6-8

2 pounds sirloin steak, cut into strips
1 can cream of mushroom soup
1 package onion soup
1 cup water
1 cup sour cream

Brown beef in nonstick skillet; add cream of mushroom soup, onion soup and water; stir until ingredients are mixed well and smooth. Simmer over medium heat until beef is tender, about 30-45 minutes. Add sour cream just before serving.

Various types of limu or seaweed grew profusely in the waters of old Kahala and Kaalawai at one time.

BREADED BEEF OR BREADED PORK CUTLETS   Serves 4-6

One of the most popular dishes at Kuhio Grill, a popular hang-out for college students, was their beef or pork cutlet with a generous portion of gravy, served with 2 scoops of rice, peas and carrots. Although this is not the original recipe from Kuhio Grill, it is another version of an old-time favorite which should evoke some great memories of the good times many had at Moiliili's famous restaurant.

6 lean beef or pork cutlets, 1/2-inch thick
Salt and pepper to taste
1 cup flour
2 eggs, slightly beaten
Canola oil for frying

Gravy:
1/4 cup fat from pan drippings
1/4 cup all-purpose flour
Beef broth or water plus beef bouillon cube
Salt and pepper to taste

Season cutlets with salt and pepper; coat with flour then dip into eggs and coat again with flour. Pan-fry in hot oil until well browned on both sides, allowing about 3-5 minutes or until cooked, on each side. Drain on paper towel and serve with gravy.

After frying cutlets, pour pan drippings into a large measuring cup to make gravy. Skim and reserve fat from drippings. Place 1/4 cup of the fat into medium saucepan (discard remaining fat); stir in flour. Add enough broth or water to remaining drippings in the measuring cup to equal 2 cups. Add all at once to flour-fat mixture and cook, stirring continuously, over medium heat until thickened and bubbly. Cook and stir additional minute. Season with salt and pepper to taste.

EVERYDAY MEATLOAF

Serves 4 to 6

3/4 cup dry bread crumbs
1 cup milk
1 1/2 pounds ground beef
2 eggs, beaten
1/4 cup grated onion
1 teaspoon salt
1/4 teaspoon sage
1/4 teaspoon pepper

Piquant Sauce:
6 tablespoons brown sugar
1/2 cup catsup
1/2 teaspoon nutmeg
2 teaspoons mustard

Soak bread crumbs in milk. Add meat, eggs, onion and seasonings; mix together well. Place in a loaf pan. Combine Piquant Sauce ingredients and spread over top of meatloaf. Bake at 350°F. 45 minutes.

Note: If you double the recipe, use a 9 x 13-inch pan and triple the sauce.

MEATLOAF ORIENTAL STYLE

Serves 6-8

2 pounds lean ground beef
1 cup panko or regular bread crumbs
2 eggs
1 onion, diced
2 teaspoons salt
1/2 cup catsup
1/4 teaspoon pepper

Sauce:
2 tablespoons brown sugar
2 tablespoons honey
2 tablespoons dry mustard
1 tablespoon vinegar
3/4 cup water
1/2 cup catsup

Combine ground beef, panko or bread crumbs, eggs, onion, salt, catsup and pepper; mix well and place in loaf pan. Bake at 350°F. 30 minutes. Combine Sauce ingredients. Remove meatloaf from oven and pour sauce over; bake for additional 30-45 minutes or until done.

HAWAIIAN TERIYAKI BURGER   Serves 6-8

1 1/2 pounds ground round
1/4 cup sugar
1 small onion, chopped
1 egg
1/4 cup soy sauce
2 cloves garlic, minced
1/2 teaspoon ginger, minced
2 tablespoons sesame oil
2 stalks green onion, chopped

Combine all ingredients and form into patties (about 1/4 pound each). Fry, grill, or broil to preference.

LONDON BROIL   Serves 6

1 3/4 pounds flank steak

Marinade:
2 teaspoons salt
1 teaspoon black pepper
1/2 teaspoon basil
1/2 teaspoon rosemary
2 cloves garlic, mashed
1 small onion, chopped
2 tablespoons white wine vinegar
1/4 cup salad oil

Soak in marinade overnight. Broil 3 inches from heat for 5 minutes or longer on each side. Cut diagonally and serve.

HAMBURGER STEAK WITH GRAVY

Serves 4

One of Hawaii's most popular dishes — it's certain to be a hit with everyone, every time!

2 slices bread, cubed
1/4 cup milk or water
1 egg, slightly beaten
1/2 cup chopped onion
1 teaspoon salt
Dash of pepper
1/4 cup tomato catsup
1 pound lean ground beef

Gravy:
2 tablespoons meat drippings (fat and juices)
2 tablespoons all-purpose flour
1 cup liquid (meat juices, broth, water)
1/4 teaspoon salt
1/4 teaspoon pepper

Mix bread cubes with milk or water until bread is softened. Mix in egg, onion, salt, pepper and catsup. Add ground beef and mix well; form into patties. Pan fry or broil to desired doneness. Serve with gravy, if desired.

Place cooked hamburgers on warm platter and keep warm while preparing Gravy. Pour drippings from pan into bowl, leaving brown particles in pan. Return 2 tablespoons drippings to pan. Stir in flour and cook over medium heat, stirring constantly, until flour is browned and mixture is smooth and bubbly; remove from heat. Stir in liquid and heat to boiling, stirring constantly. Boil and stir 1 minute. Stir in few drops of browning sauce, if desired. Add salt and pepper. Makes 1 cup gravy.

Variation:
Loco Moco: Serve the hamburger steak on a bed of hot, steamed rice with eggs "over easy" and smothered with gravy.

ITALIAN CASSEROLE
Serves 6

1 large eggplant
1 egg, beaten
3 tablespoons oil
3 ounces pepperoni, sliced and cut into 1/4-inch strips
1 pound ground beef
2 medium onions, chopped
1 can (No. 303) tomato puree
1/8 teaspoon basil
1/8 teaspoon oregano
1/2 cup green pepper, chopped
1 teaspoon salt
Dash of pepper
1 clove garlic, crushed
1/2 pound mozzarella cheese, coarsely grated

Peel and slice eggplant into 1/4-inch slices; dip in egg and sauté in hot oil until browned; drain. Sauté pepperoni; remove and set aside. Sauté beef, add onions and cook over medium heat until soft. Add puree, basil, oregano, green pepper, salt, pepper and garlic. Divide eggplant, meat mixture, pepperoni and cheese into thirds; arrange 1/3 of eggplant in nonstick 3 quart casserole or oblong cake pan. Top with layers of meat mixture, pepperoni and cheese. Make 3 layers. Bake, uncovered, at 350°F. 1 hour.

Mrs. Joyce Fasi
Wife of Former Mayor Frank F. Fasi
City and County of Honolulu

In the early 1920s, a clean pocket of pure white sand, which evidences the thought that there was some connection between this area and the sea once upon a time, was discovered near the foothills of St. Louis Heights

MEAT JUN

1 pound sirloin tip, teriyaki or flank steak, sliced
3/4 cup flour
3 eggs, beaten
1/4 cup salad oil for frying

Marinade:
1/2 cup shoyu
1/4 cup sugar
1/4 cup minced green onions
2 cloves garlic, grated
1 tablespoon sesame seeds
1 1/2 teaspoon sesame oil
1/4 teaspoon pepper

Soak beef in the Marinade for at least 1 hour in the refrigerator. Dredge meat in flour, then dip into beaten eggs. Fry in hot oil on both sides. Drain on paper towel. Slice and serve.

TAMAGO HAMBURGER CASSEROLE

1 pound ground beef
2 teaspoons canola oil
1/2 onion, chopped
1 teaspoon sugar
Dash of salt
1 teaspoon soy sauce
2 cups boiling water
1/2 package of dashi-no-moto or dried shrimp
2 or more eggs
Pickled red ginger to taste

Fry ground beef in hot oil until brown. Add onion, sugar, salt and soy sauce. If taste isn't to your liking, add more or use less seasoning. Add water boiled with dashi-no-moto or dried shrimp to just cover beef mixture; simmer. In separate bowl, mix eggs with salt to taste, 1 tablespoon water for each egg. Slowly pour eggs over hamburger in pan; cover and simmer until eggs set. Pour over hot rice. Sprinkle red ginger over all.

TOFU MEATLOAF
Serves 6

1 block firm tofu, drained and mashed
2 pounds ground beef
l envelope onion-mushroom dry soup mix
2 eggs
1/4 cup minced green pepper, optional
1/2 cup dry bread crumbs
1/4 cup brown sugar
1/4 cup shoyu
1 teaspoon prepared mustard

In large bowl, mix together tofu, beef, soup mix, eggs, optional green pepper and bread crumbs. Place into 9-inch round casserole dish. Bake for 30 minutes at 350°. In sauce pan, combine sugar and shoyu, cook over low heat until sugar is dissolved. Stir in mustard. Drizzle sauce over meatloaf. Bake additional 10-15 minutes.

VEAL PARMIGIANO

Serves 4-6

3 cloves garlic, minced
1 onion, minced
6 tablespoons olive oil
1 1/4 teaspoons salt
1/4 teaspoon pepper
1 can (No. 2) whole tomatoes
1 can (8 oz.) tomato sauce
1 can mushroom pieces
4 teaspoons thyme
1/2 teaspoon oregano
1 - 2 eggs
1/4 cup dried bread crumbs
1/4 cup Parmesan cheese
1 to 2 pounds veal steak, thin slices
1/4 -1/3 cup Romano or Parmesan cheese
1 package mozzarella cheese, sliced thin

Sauté garlic and onion in 3 tablespoons olive oil until golden brown. Add salt, pepper and whole tomatoes; mash tomatoes with spoon; simmer 10 minutes. Add tomato sauce, mushrooms, thyme and oregano; simmer 20 minutes. Taste as you go along. Beat eggs with a fork; set aside. Combine bread crumbs and Parmesan cheese. Dip veal slices in beaten eggs and then in bread crumb mixture; sauté in remaining olive oil until golden brown.

In a 12 x 8 x 2-inch baking dish, place veal side by side; spoon half of the tomato mixture over veal, then arrange Mozzarella cheese over top. Spoon remaining tomato mixture on and sprinkle with Romano or Parmesan cheese. Bake at 350°F. 30 minutes.

Mrs. Joyce Fasi,
Wife of Former Mayor Frank F. Fasi
City and County of Honolulu

WIENERSCHNITZEL

2 pounds veal cutlet, sliced thin
1/2 cup flour
1 teaspoon salt
1 teaspoon pepper
1/2 teaspoon paprika
1 egg, beaten
2/3 cup milk
Bread crumbs
3 tablespoons olive oil
1 tablespoon butter

If veal cutlets are not very thin, place chop between two sheets of plastic wrap and pound to about 3/8-inch thickness. Mix together flour, salt, pepper and paprika. In separate bowl, mix together egg and milk. Dip each piece of veal in flour mixture, then egg mixture, then bread crumbs. Fry cutlets in oil and butter mixture, heated until sizzling, until golden brown on both sides. Drain on absorbent paper. Serve with sauerkraut or mashed potatoes.

MEATS - PORK

BAKED HAM
Serves 25

    6 pounds canned ham
    3/4 tablespoon whole cloves
    1/2 cup canned pineapple juice
    3/4 cup brown sugar, packed

Place ham in baking pan, fat side up. Pour natural jelly from can over ham; score ham and stud with cloves. Mix together pineapple juice and sugar; mix well and pour over ham. Bake at 325°F. 90 minutes (allow 15 minutes per pound) or until internal temperature of ham reaches 130°F. Baste frequently while baking.

Note: To cut baking time in half and to eliminate basting, an oven roasting bag may be used (follow box directions).

GOLDEN HAM CASSEROLE
Serves 6

    2 cups cubed ham
    2 tablespoons chopped onion
    1/4 cup butter
    2 cups partially cooked potatoes, cubed
    1 cup partially cooked celery, diced
    2 tablespoons chopped green pepper
    3 tablespoons butter
    2 tablespoons flour
    1-1/2 cup milk
    1 teaspoon salt
    Dash pepper
    1/2 cup grated cheese
    1/2 cup buttered bread crumbs

Brown ham and onion in butter. Arrange layers of ham and vegetables in buttered casserole dish. In saucepan, melt the 3 tablespoons butter; stir in flour. Add milk, seasonings and cheese. Cook over low heat until slightly thickened. Pour over ham and vegetables. Sprinkle with bread crumbs. Bake at 375°F. 25-30 minutes.

GRANDMA'S TOFU (MAPO TOFU)   Serves 4

- 1 tablespoon vegetable oil
- 1/4 pound ground beef or pork
- 1 teaspoon minced garlic
- 1 teaspoon minced ginger
- 1 teaspoon hot bean paste
- 1 1/2 tablespoons soy sauce
- 1 cup chicken broth
- 1/2 block tofu, diced
- 2 teaspoons cornstarch
- 2 teaspoons water
- 1 teaspoon sesame oil
- 2 tablespoons minced green onion

Stir-fry meat in hot oil 1 minute. Add garlic, ginger, hot bean paste, soy sauce, chicken broth and tofu. Bring to a boil over high heat and cook 2 minutes over medium heat. Mix cornstarch and water to make paste; add to meat mixture and cook until thickened. Add sesame oil and sprinkle with green onion before serving.

Robert Hsu, Owner/Manager
Maple Garden Restaurant

Moiliili Hongwanji Church has served the Buddhists of the Moiliili area since 1906. The present building was constructed in 1960.

HAWAIIAN STYLE SPARERIBS
Serves 4-6

2-3 pounds spareribs
1/2 cup brown sugar, packed
1/2 cup catsup
2 tablespoons soy sauce
1 tablespoon white vinegar
1 tablespoon flour
1/2 teaspoon powdered ginger
1 teaspoon salt
1 large clove garlic, mashed

Place spareribs in baking dish. Combine remaining ingredients and mix well; pour mixture over ribs, making certain that each rib is well marinated. Bake, turning ribs over once after 30 minutes, at 350°F. 1 hour or until done.

INDONESIAN PORK ROAST
Serves 6

3 pounds pork butt
1 clove garlic
1 cube chicken bouillon
1/3 cup vinegar
1/4 cup water
1/2 cup shoyu

Brown pork on all sides in a large pan. Combine remaining ingredients and pour over pork. Simmer for 3 hours. Shred pork with a fork before serving.

Leatrice Chee
Vice-Principal
Kaimuki High School

MUSHROOM STUFFED PORK CHOPS

Serves 4

8 small sized boneless pork chops
1 tablespoon olive oil
1 tablespoon butter
**1/2 pound shiitake mushrooms, stems removed and
    chopped**
**1/2 pound portabella mushrooms, stems removed and
    chopped**
2 tablespoons minced garlic
1 1/2 cup flour, for dredging
2 eggs, beaten for egg wash
1 cup bread crumbs
Salt and pepper

Cut each pork chop in the middle to create a pocket;
sprinkle with salt and pepper and put on the side. In a
sauté pan, heat the oil and butter at a medium/high heat;
add chopped mushrooms and garlic. Sauté for 10 to 15
minutes or until mushrooms soften; add salt and pepper to
taste. Stuff each pork chop with approximately 2 spoonfuls
of sautéed mushrooms. Dredge pork chops in flour, dip
into the egg wash and roll in bread crumbs. Bake at 350°F
30 minutes or until done. Serve with tonkatsu sauce.

Former Governor & Mrs. George R. Ariyoshi

*The stone quarry, owned and operated by Honolulu
Construction and Dredging (HC&D), provided jobs for
many until the late 1940's when it was closed. It is now
the site of the University of Hawaii's Sports Arena, park-
ing structure, classrooms and dorms.*

ONO SPARERIBS

Serves 4-6

5 pounds country style spareribs
2-inch piece fresh ginger, crushed

Sauce:
3/4 cup sugar
1 cup catsup
1/3 cup oyster sauce
3/4 cup soy sauce
Wine to taste, optional

Place spareribs in large pot with ginger; add water to cover. Cover and simmer for 30 minutes or until tender; drain and cool. Combine Sauce ingredients and pour over spareribs; bring mixture to a boil and simmer on low heat 1-1 1/2 hours or until very tender.

PORK ADOBO

Serves 4-6

2 pounds pork (leg, shoulder, butt or belly), cut into 1-inch cubes
1 teaspoon whole peppercorns, cracked
2 bay leaves, broken in half
1 whole head garlic, minced or crushed
3/4 cup cider vinegar
1/4 cup soy sauce

Sauté pork on high heat in medium saucepan until brown on all sides. Add remaining ingredients; bring to a boil, lower heat to medium-low and cook 20-30 minutes. Reduce heat to low and simmer about 30-45 minutes, stirring occasionally, until pork is tender and gravy thickens. Pour off excess oil before serving. Serve with hot steamed rice.

Variation:
Chicken may be substituted for pork, if desired.

PORK HASH MEAT LOAF

Serves 8-10

"Here's a simple dish great for tailgating or gathering of friends and family...it's ono!"

- **1 pound lean ground pork**
- **2 pounds lean ground beef**
- **1 medium round onion, minced**
- **1 cup bread crumbs**
- **2 eggs, beaten**
- **3 ounces fresh mushrooms, sliced thinly**
- **1/2 cup raw honey**
- **1 teaspoon salt**
- **1 teaspoon pepper**
- **1 bottle (3 oz.) pimento**

Combine all ingredients in a large bowl; mix well. Place in lightly greased or nonstick loaf pan or casserole dish and bake at 350°F. 60-70 minutes or until done. Drain drippings, add flour and whip or add 1 can (10.75 oz.) cream of mushroom soup and heat slowly for your gravy.

Hari Kojima, TV2 Host
Hari's Kitchen and
Let's Go Fishing

The Honolulu Stadium was the site of high school and University sports events, Hula Bowls, Islander baseball games, stock car races, Boy Scout Makahikis, bon dances and other festivities for more than 50 years. It was demolished in January, 1976.

SHOYU BONELESS PORK BUTT

"An excellent dish that I like to cook on Sundays... got this a long time ago from a former mother-in-law. Thanks, Grandma!"

1 piece (5-6 pounds) boneless pork butt (or, if on sale, the one with bone is okay too!)

Sauce:
1 cup soy sauce
2/3 cup sugar
1 piece (thumb size) fresh ginger, crushed
2 cloves garlic, crushed
1/2 cup water
1/8 teaspoon sesame oil
1 tablespoon Scotch whiskey

Brown pork evenly on all sides in large, heavy pot; pour out excess oil. Combine all ingredients for the Sauce and pour over pork; bring to a boil and reduce heat to low. Cover and simmer for 2-2 1/2 hours, turning pork over on all sides during cooking.

Hari Kojima, TV2 Host
Hari's Kitchen and
Let's Go Fishing

SWEET SOUR SPARERIBS

1 1/2-2 pounds spareribs, chopped
1/2 cup flour
1/3 cup soy sauce
1 tablespoon canola oil
1 clove garlic, crushed
1 piece (1-inch) fresh ginger, crushed
1/3 cup vinegar
3/4 cup water
1/2 cup brown sugar, packed
1 teaspoon salt

Mix flour and soy sauce to make paste; marinate spareribs in mixture for about 30 minutes. Heat oil; add garlic, ginger and ribs; brown. Add vinegar, water, sugar and salt; simmer over low heat for about 1 hour or until ribs are tender. Serve on bed of pickled turnips and carrots.

TAIWAN MUSHI
(Pork-Tofu Casserole)
Serves 6-8

1 pound lean ground pork
1 teaspoon salad oil
8 medium dried mushrooms, soaked in water until softened and cut into strips
1 medium round onion, sliced
1 small can (8 oz.) water chestnuts, drained and chopped
2 tablespoons sake
1/4 teaspoon salt
1/4 cup soy sauce
2 tablespoons sugar
1 block firm tofu, cut into 1-inch cubes
2 large eggs, beaten

Fry pork in hot oil; add mushrooms, onions and water chestnuts; sauté until pork is browned. Add sake, salt, soy sauce and sugar; stir to mix well. Place tofu cubes in bottom of nonstick 9 x 13-inch baking pan or 3-quart glass casserole dish; pour pork mixture over tofu. Pour eggs evenly over pork mixture; cover and bake at 350°F. 35 minutes.

Many came to Moiliili to view the sumo bouts at the Kashiwabara dohyo.

TANGY FRANKS BARBECUE

Serves 5

2 tablespoons prepared mustard
2 cans (8 oz. each) tomato sauce
1/2 cup dark corn syrup
1/3 cup vinegar
1/3 cup minced onion
2 tablespoons Worcestershire sauce
1/4 -1/2 teaspoon bottled hot pepper sauce, optional
1 pound franks

Combine all ingredients, except franks, in a saucepan and simmer over low heat 30 minutes. Add franks; simmer additional 8-10 minutes or until franks are plump.

POULTRY

APRICOT CHICKEN

Serves 4-6

2 pounds chicken wings, washed and cut into serving pieces
Salt and pepper to taste
1 jar (18 oz.) apricot preserves

Season chicken with salt and pepper; arrange on broiler pan and broil until light brown on both sides. Remove from broiler and coat with apricot preserves. Return to broiler and broil both sides until crisp.

WAIOLI FRIED CHICKEN

Serves 2

2 broiler chicken halves
1 cup flour
2 teaspoons salt
1 1/2 teaspoons monosodium glutamate, optional
1/4 teaspoon pepper
1 egg, beaten
1/2 cup milk
1 1/2 cups bread crumbs
1/4 cup shortening
1/4 cup butter

Rinse chicken and pat dry. Combine salt, monosodium glutamate, pepper and flour in paper bag; shake to mix well. Place chicken in bag; shake vigorously; remove and dip in mixture of egg and milk. Roll in crumbs. Fry in hot mixture of shortening and butter until brown on both sides. Place in heavy pan with 2 tablespoons water; cover tightly and bake at 350°F. 50-60 minutes.

The Original Waioli Tea Room Restaurant (1974)

BAKED CHICKEN WITH RICE

Serves 8-10

This casserole is an easy "meal-in-one" dish to prepare. It never fails and is delicious!

3 cups converted rice (ie. Uncle Ben's)
5 pounds chicken thighs
Salt and pepper to taste
1/4 teaspoon garlic powder
3 cans water
1 can cream of celery soup
1 can cream of mushroom soup
1 package (16 oz.) frozen peas, peas and carrots or
mixed vegetables.

Sprinkle rice evenly in nonstick casserole dish or 9 x 13-inch pan. Sprinkle chicken with salt, pepper and garlic powder; arrange over rice and set aside. Add frozen vegetables as desired. Stir water with soups until well mixed; pour over chicken. Cover and bake at 375°F. 1 1/2-2 hours or until chicken is cooked.

Mrs. Joyce Fasi
Wife of Former Mayor Frank Fasi
City and County of Honolulu

BAKED MAYONNAISE CHICKEN

Serves 4-6

2-3 pounds boneless chicken breasts or thighs
1/2 cup mayonnaise
1 1/2 teaspoon salt
Dash of pepper
1/4 teaspoon garlic salt
1 cup corn flakes, crushed

Wash and dry chicken. Combine mayonnaise, salt, pepper and garlic salt. Coat chicken with mixture, then roll in crushed corn flakes. Bake at 400°F. 25 minutes, then lower temperature to 350°F. and bake for an additional 20 minutes.

BARBECUED CHICKEN
Serves 6-8

Sauce:
3/4 cup soy sauce
2 tablespoons honey
1/2 cup brown sugar, packed
2 tablespoons fresh ginger, minced
1 1/2 cups water
1/4 cup minced green onions
3 cloves garlic, minced
1 pinch star anise
2 tablespoons sherry wine

5 pounds chicken thighs
2 tablespoons cornstarch
1/4 cup water

Combine Sauce ingredients in large pot and cook over medium heat 5-10 minutes. Add chicken and continue cooking for about 45 minutes. Just before serving, combine cornstarch with water to make a paste; add to chicken mixture and cook until thickened.

Moiliili is supported by vast underground caverns of water. In years past, several places in Moiliili sank and there were numerous holes - one behind the Kanda Store on King Street and beneath the Kamada duplex in Kalo Lane as well as one close to the makai side of the University Avenue-South King Street intersection.

BARBECUED FRIED CHICKEN NO. 1   Serves 4-6

3-4 pounds chicken parts or wings
1/4 cup flour
1 cup canola or vegetable oil

Sauce:
1/2 cup sugar
1/2 cup soy sauce
1/4 cup minced green onion
2 cloves garlic, minced
2 tablespoons fresh ginger, minced

Coat chicken with flour and deep fry in hot oil until brown on both sides. Stir Sauce ingredients together then dip fried chicken pieces to serve.

BARBECUED FRIED CHICKEN NO. 2   Serves 4-6

Barbecue Sauce:
1 cup sugar
1/2 cup soy sauce

3 pounds fryer chicken, cut into serving pieces
2 eggs, well beaten
1/2 cup flour
2 cups canola or vegetable oil for frying

Prepare Barbecue Sauce by cooking sugar and soy sauce together until sugar dissolves. Set aside.

Dip chicken pieces in beaten eggs then roll in flour until well coated. Deep fry in oil heated to 350°F. until brown on both sides; drain on absorbent paper and dip in Barbecue Sauce while hot.

BROILED CHICKEN WITH
VINEGAR AND HONEY

Serves 2-3

Sauce:
3 tablespoons cider vinegar
1 tablespoon honey
2 cloves garlic, minced
2 teaspoons fresh ginger, minced
2 teaspoons soy sauce
1 teaspoon Dijon mustard

1 whole chicken (2 1/2-3 lbs. fryer), split lengthwise

Combine Sauce ingredients in blender or food processor and blend 10-15 minutes. Brush chicken well with Sauce. Broil, skin side down, on greased or sprayed rack in a 13 x 9 x 2-inch pan for 10 minutes; turn and continue broiling for additional 10 minutes. Transfer chicken to 400°F. oven. Roast, uncovered, basting occasionally with remainder of Sauce for 20-25 minutes or until done. Cover chicken with foil if it browns too quickly.

CHICKEN NOODLE CHICKEN

Serves 4-6

2 pounds chicken thighs
2 cans (10.75 oz.) chicken noodle soup
Salt and pepper to taste
1/2 teaspoon dried oregano

Arrange chicken in nonstick baking dish and pour soup over. Sprinkle with salt, pepper and oregano. Bake at 350°F. 1 hour or until done.

> *Moiliili Community Center stands on land which housed Kihachi Kashiwabara's Japanese Language School*

81

CHICKEN AJITSUKE
Serves 4

2 pounds chicken thighs, deboned and cut into bite sizes

Marinade:
1 stalk green onion, chopped
1 small egg, beaten
1 teaspoon salt
1 tablespoon oyster sauce
1 tablespoon catsup
1 teaspoon sugar
1 tablespoon sake
1 clove garlic, pressed or crushed
1/2 teaspoon grated fresh ginger
1/2 cup katakuriko or cornstarch
1/2 cup flour
1 quart canola oil for frying

Mix together Marinade ingredients and marinate chicken for 1 hour or more. Roll chicken in katakuriko and flour mixture. Deep fry in hot oil over medium heat 5-6 minutes or until golden brown and done. Drain on absorbent paper before serving. Chicken may be served hot or cold — also good as a sandwich filling.

Note: Double the Marinade recipe if cooking more chicken.

CHICKEN CHILI
Serves 10-15

If you don't tell anyone it's chicken, they won't even know the difference!

2 pounds ground chicken
2 onions, diced
4 cloves garlic, minced
1 can (14.5 oz.) diced stewed tomatoes
2 cans (8 oz. each) tomato sauce
2 cans (14.5 oz.) red kidney beans

5 tablespoons chili powder
2 teaspoons garlic salt
2 teaspoons oregano
2 teaspoons cumin
2 teaspoons black pepper
1 teaspoon crushed red pepper
1/2 teaspoon cayenne pepper

Brown chicken in a large pot; add onions and garlic and cook until onions are soft. Add all other ingredients and simmer 2 hours, stirring occasionally.

Note: This chili is on the spicy side. For milder chili, reduce or eliminate red and cayenne peppers.

CHICKEN CURRY   Serves 4-6

4 slices bacon, chopped
1/4 cup celery, sliced
1/4 cup onion, chopped
1 clove garlic
2 tablespoons flour
1 cup milk
1 cup water
1/2 cup applesauce
3 teaspoons tomato paste
3-4 teaspoons curry powder
2 cubes chicken bouillon
3 cups cooked chicken, cubed

Fry bacon; add celery, onions and garlic. Add flour, milk, water, applesauce, tomato paste, curry powder and bouillon. Add cubed chicken and cook over low heat 20 minutes.

Judith Saranchock
Principal
Ala Wai School

CHICKEN IN-A-HURRY

Serves 4-6

> **2 pounds boneless, skinless chicken thighs**
> **1 cup flour**
> **Salt and pepper to taste**
> **Paprika to taste**
> **1/2 cup butter**
> **1 jar (6 oz.) artichokes**
> **1/2 cup sake or sherry**
> **1 can (10.75 oz.) cream of mushroom soup**

Coat chicken in mixture of flour, salt, pepper and paprika. Brown in butter and liquid from jar of artichoke. Add sake or sherry and simmer about 20 minutes or until chicken is tender. Add water, if necessary.

Add cream of mushroom soup and artichoke hearts; continue cooking for about 10 minutes. Serve with steamed rice or potatoes.

CHICKEN WITH MUSHROOMS

Serves 2-4

> **1 pound boneless chicken thighs, cut into bite size pieces**
> **2 tablespoons canola or salad oil**
> **1 can (No. 303) straw mushrooms or 8 dried mushrooms, soaked in water to soften**
> **1/2 cup bamboo shoots, sliced**
> **1/4 cup chopped green onions**
> **Chinese parsley or Chinese peas for garnish**
>
> **Marinade:**
> **1 tablespoon sherry or mirin**
> **Pepper to taste**
> **1 tablespoon oyster sauce**
>
> **Gravy:**
> **1 1/2 teaspoons cornstarch**
> **1/2 teaspoon sugar**
> **1/4 teaspoon pepper**
> **1/2 cup chicken broth**
> **1 tablespoon soy sauce**

Mix together Marinade ingredients and soak chicken just before cooking, about 5-10 minutes. Stir-fry chicken in 1 tablespoon hot oil; remove from pan just before chicken is cooked. Sauté mushrooms and bamboo shoots in remaining 1 tablespoon oil; return chicken to pan. Mix together Gravy ingredients and pour over chicken. Cook until gravy comes to a boil. Garnish with green onions and parsley or Chinese peas.

FAST AND SIMPLE CHICKEN CURRY   Serves 6-8

2 pounds chicken thighs, deboned and cut into bite size
    pieces
1 cup chopped onions
2 cloves garlic, crushed
1 tablespoon canola oil
1 1/2 cups chicken broth
1 2/3 cups evaporated milk, undiluted
3/4 cup water
1/4 cup cornstarch
2 tablespoons curry powder
1/2 teaspoon cumin
1/2 teaspoon salt
1/4 teaspoon pepper

Sauté chicken, onion and garlic in hot oil. Stir in chicken broth, evaporated milk and 1/2 cup water. Combine remaining 1/4 cup water with cornstarch; stir until smooth and stir into broth mixture. Add curry powder, cumin, salt and pepper. Cook over medium heat, stirring occasionally, until mixture comes to a boil and thickens. Serve over steamed rice. If desired, your favorite condiments may be served with the curry.

FRIED CHICKEN DRUMMETTES

Serves 6-10

Dipping Sauce:
1/2 cup soy sauce
1 clove garlic, minced
3 tablespoons sugar
2 drops sesame oil
1 teaspoon Togarashi (Oriental hot pepper)
1 stalk green onion, minced

5 pounds chicken drummettes
2 eggs, well beaten
1 cup flour
1/2 gallon canola or vegetable oil for frying

Mix together all ingredients for Dipping Sauce; set aside. Dip chicken in beaten eggs, then roll in flour until well coated. Deep fry in 375°F. oil until browned; drain on absorbent paper. While hot, dip into Dipping Sauce.

ITALIAN CHICKEN

Serves 8

2-3 pounds boneless chicken
1/2 cup flour
1/4 cup olive oil
2 jars (6 oz. each) marinated artichokes
2 cans (16 oz. each) whole tomatoes, drained
4 cloves garlic, minced
1 pound fresh mushrooms, sliced
1 cup sherry
1 1/2 teaspoons salt
3/4 teaspoon pepper
1 teaspoon oregano
2 teaspoons basil

Lightly flour chicken; brown in hot olive oil and add liquid from artichokes. Put chicken in casserole dish. Mix together remaining ingredients, except artichokes, and pour over chicken. Bake uncovered at 350°F. 50 minutes. Add artichokes and bake additional 10 minutes.

GOVERNOR CAYETANO'S
FAVORITE CHICKEN ADOBO

Serves 6-8

3 pounds chicken thighs, cut into serving pieces
1/2 cup white vinegar
1/2 cup soy sauce
1/4 cup peppercorns, crushed
1 teaspoon brown sugar
5 cloves garlic, crushed
3 bay leaves
Salt to taste

Combine all ingredients in a pan; cover and allow to marinate 1-3 hours. Bring to a boil, then lower heat and simmer for 30 minutes. Uncover the pan and allow to simmer for an additional 15 minutes or until most of the liquid has evaporated and the chicken is lightly brown. Serve with steamed white rice.

Benjamin J. Cayetano
Governor
State of Hawaii

TERI YAKITORI

Serves 4-6

1 pound boneless chicken
1/3 cup soy sauce
1/4 cup sugar
1 clove garlic, crushed
1 small piece fresh ginger root, crushed
Bamboo skewers

Remove skin from chicken and cut into 1-inch pieces. Thread 3-4 pieces of chicken on each bamboo skewer. Combine soy sauce, sugar, garlic and ginger and marinate skewered chicken for at least 30 minutes before grilling. Grill on outdoor grill or broil in oven-broiler until done.

KORAKU'S KOREAN-STYLE
BARBECUE CHICKEN

Serves 2-4

3/4 cup soy sauce
1/2 cup sugar
1 tablespoon shaved ginger
5 cloves garlic, crushed
2 tablespoons sesame oil
1 1/2 teaspoons sesame seeds
1/2 teaspoon black pepper
2 tablespoons chopped green onions
1 pound boneless chicken thighs

In mixing bowl, combine all ingredients except chicken. Place chicken in shallow baking pan and pour mixture over all pieces. Soak chicken in marinade for at least 2 hours. Grill and serve.

Koraku Restaurant

KOREAN STYLE BARBECUE CHICKEN

Serves 4-6

2-3 pounds chicken, cut into serving pieces

Sauce:
1/2 cup soy sauce
1/2 cup sugar
1/4 cup sake
1 teaspoon salt
1 tablespoon sesame oil
1 teaspoon toasted sesame seeds
1 slice fresh ginger, crushed
1 clove garlic, crushed

Combine Sauce ingredients and marinate chicken 1-2 hours. Place in saucepan, cover and bring to a boil. Continue cooking on low heat, turning once, 30 minutes or until tender and done. If desired, chicken may be broiled or grilled instead, turning over once during cooking, until brown on both sides and done.

MISO CHICKEN
Serves 10-12

5 pounds boneless chicken thighs
3/4 cup soy sauce
3/4 cup sugar
3/4 cup miso
3/4 cup beer

Combine ingredients and marinate overnight. Broil over charcoal or in oven until done.

Leatrice Chee
Vice-Principal
Kaimuki High School

MOCHIKO CHICKEN
Serves 4-6

2 pounds chicken thighs, deboned
1/4 cup mochiko
1/4 cup cornstarch
1/4 cup sugar
5 tablespoons soy sauce
1/4 cup minced green onions
2 eggs, beaten
2 cloves garlic, minced
1/2 teaspoon salt

Mix together all ingredients, except chicken, in large bowl; marinate chicken in mixture 2-12 hours. Deep fry or pan fry chicken in hot oil until browned and cooked. Drain on absorbent paper before serving.

Note: For 5 pounds of chicken thighs, double recipe and soak chicken overnight.

MRS. AOKI'S SHOYU CHICKEN   Serves 4

Very simple and delicious!

>   **2 pounds chicken wings or thighs**
>   **1/4 cup corn oil**
>   **1/4 cup soy sauce**
>   **1/4 cup brown or white sugar**
>   **1 clove garlic, crushed**
>   **1/2 teaspoon grated fresh ginger**

Mix together oil, soy sauce, sugar, garlic and ginger. Add chicken and bake in aluminum foil lined pan at 325°F. 1 hour, turning twice. Before serving, sauce may be thickened with cornstarch, if desired.

Note: When in a hurry, combine all the ingredients in a saucepan; cover and bring sauce to a boil. Reduce heat to low and cook 30-45 minutes or until chicken is tender and done.

PEANUT BUTTER CHICKEN   Serves 8-10

This is a great dish for picnics or barbecues!

>   **5 pounds boneless skinless chicken thighs**
>   **1 cup sugar**
>   **1 cup soy sauce**
>   **1 tablespoon garlic chili sauce**
>   **1 tablespoon creamy peanut butter**
>   **1 tablespoon white miso**
>   **2 tablespoons mirin**
>   **1/2 cup chopped green onion**
>   **6 cloves garlic, pressed**
>   **6 slices ginger, pressed**

Combine all ingredients and marinate chicken 4-6 hours. Barbecue over hot coals.

SWEET SOUR CHICKEN THIGHS
Serves 4

2 pounds chicken thighs, deboned and skin removed
2 tablespoons cornstarch
1/4 cup soy sauce
1 teaspoon salt
2 tablespoons grated fresh ginger
2 tablespoons garlic puree

Sauce:
3/4 cup brown sugar, packed
1/3 cup vinegar
3/4 cup water

Combine cornstarch, soy sauce, salt, ginger and garlic; mix well and marinate chicken for 1 hour. Brown in frying pan filled with hot oil; remove and place in another pot. Combine Sauce ingredients; mix well and pour mixture over chicken. Bring Sauce to a boil and simmer over low heat for 1 hour or until chicken is tender.

BAKED MACARONI WITH CHICKEN
Serves 4-6

1 whole chicken, boiled and shredded
1 can (10.75 oz.) cream of mushroom soup
1 package (10 oz.) frozen peas and carrots, rinsed
2 cups cooked macaroni
2 stalks celery, chopped
1 small round onion, chopped
2 tablespoons butter
1/2 teaspoon salt
1/2 teaspoon curry powder
3 tablespoons mayonnaise
1 cup milk
1/2 teaspoon black pepper
1 teaspoon sherry wine
1/2 cup chicken broth

Mix all above ingredients and place into a 3 quart casserole dish. Bake at 350°F. 40-45 minutes.

FISH & SEAFOODS

BAKED MAHI
Serves 4

> **2 pounds mahimahi, cut into pieces about 3 inches wide**
> **Salt and pepper to taste**
> **1 cup mayonnaise**
> **1/2 cup grated parmesan cheese**
> **1/2 cup round onion, finely chopped**

Wash and dry mahi; sprinkle both sides with salt and pepper. Bake at 325°F. 10 minutes on each side or until cooked. Combine mayonnaise and parmesan cheese and spread on top of cooked mahi; sprinkle with onion. Broil about 10 minutes to brown top.

BARBECUE AHI TEMPURA
Serves 4-6

> **2 pounds ahi filet, sliced in 2-inch squares**
> **Flour to coat fish**
> **Canola oil for frying**
>
> **Sauce:**
> **1/3 cup soy sauce**
> **1/3 cup sugar**
> **1/4 cup water**
> **1/2 teaspoon sesame oil**
> **1 teaspoon chives, chopped fine**
> **1 tablespoon green onion, chopped**
> **2 cloves garlic, minced**
> **1/3 finger fresh ginger, grated**
>
> **Batter:**
> **1/2 cup flour**
> **2 teaspoons salt**
> **2 eggs, beaten**
> **1/2 cup water-add more as needed for desired**
> **   consistency**

Combine Sauce ingredients day before; marinate fish in Sauce 2-12 hours. Prepare batter by combining flour and salt, then add eggs and milk; stir to combine; set aside. Coat fish with flour; dip in batter and fry in 1-inch depth of hot oil. Brown both sides; drain on absorbent paper before serving.

PAN FRIED MULLET   Serves 2

1-1 1/2 pound mullet
1 package (9 oz.) chop suey vegetable mix
2 tablespoons minced ginger
4 tablespoons soy sauce
4 tablespoons oyster sauce
1/2 can (4 oz.) chicken broth
1 tablespoon cornstarch
2 tablespoons water
Salt and pepper to taste
2 tablespoons thinly sliced green onions
1/4 cup salad oil

Heat oil in a wok or deep frying pan until smoking. Score the mullet on both sides (cut 1/2-inch deep cuts every inch) and season with salt, pepper and ginger. Place seasoned mullet in hot oil and cook about 4 minutes on each side. Remove from pan. Drain all but 2 tablespoons of oil from pan. Add chop suey mix to pan. Add chicken broth, soy sauce, oyster sauce and bring to a boil. Mix cornstarch with water until smooth; add to broth mixture to thicken. Pour vegetables over fish and top with green onions. Enjoy!

Sam Choy, Owner/Chef
Sam Choy's Diamond Head Restaurant &
Sam Choy's Breakfast, Lunch & Crab

HAWAII KAI BOUILLABAISSE

Serves 4-6

1/2 pound bacon, cut in 1/2-inch pieces
1/4 cup olive oil
1 large onion, diced
4 cloves garlic, minced
1 medium bunch celery, chopped to 1/2-inch pieces
3 cans (6.5 oz. each) chopped clams with juice
1 large can (16 oz.) tomatoes, crushed
1/2 package dried onion soup
2 tablespoons basil leaves
2 bay leaves, broken in half
1 teaspoon marjoram
1 pound mahimahi filets
Salt and pepper to taste
1/2 cup flour
1/2 cup white wine, optional

Sauté bacon pieces in Dutch oven until just starting to crisp; remove from pan and drain on paper towels; set aside. Discard bacon drippings leaving residue in pan; add 1 tablespoon olive oil and sauté onions, garlic and celery on medium heat. When onions begin to brown, add clams with juice, tomatoes, onion soup, bacon, basil, bay leaves and marjoram. Stir well and simmer on low heat for at least one hour.

While bouillabaisse is simmering, cut mahimahi into 1-inch cubes and sprinkle with salt and pepper. Dredge fish in flour and sauté in remaining olive oil until fish just begins to brown on all sides. Remove from pan and drain on absorbent paper. Add fish to bouillabaisse during last 5 to 10 minutes of cooking. If bouillabaisse is too thick, add white wine. Serve with hot French bread and salad.

> *Prior to 1926, the Stadium Park area housed kiawe trees, a herd of cattle, a few homes and honey bees.*

POACHED FISH

Serves 2-3

The bones of whole fish add flavor to the fish and keep it moist, and the skin of most fish has an underlying layer of fat that seeps into the fish as it cooks to give it that added richness.

> **Water or fish stock**
> **1/4 cup minced onion**
> **2 medium whole fish (opakapaka, mullet, flounder),**
>   **scaled and cleaned**
> **1/4 cup thinly sliced green onion**
> **1 slice (1-inch) fresh ginger, grated**
> **1/4 cup canola oil, heated**
> **2 tablespoons soy sauce**

Fill a medium skillet half full with water. Add onion; cover and bring to a boil over high heat. Add fish and additional water, if necessary, so that fish is completely covered with water. Cover and bring water to a boil again. Immediately remove skillet from heat and allow fish to remain in water for 25-30 minutes or until cooked. Carefully remove fish from water with a wide spatula and arrange on serving platter. Sprinkle with green onion and grated ginger. Pour hot oil and soy sauce over fish and serve immediately.

SHRIMP PATTIES

Serves 4-6

> **1 pound shrimp, cleaned and chopped**
> **1 medium potato, peeled and grated**
> **2 tablespoons cornstarch**
> **1 egg, beaten**
> **1 gobo, chopped and soaked**
> **2 teaspoons sugar**
> **Salt to taste**
> **Oil for deep frying**

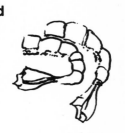

Combine all ingredients in bowl; mix well. Form into patties and deep fry in oil heated to 350°F. until done. Drain on absorbent paper before serving.

SALMON PATTIES
Serves 4

1 can (16 oz.) salmon, drained
1/2 cup green onions, chopped
1/4 cup parsley, chopped
1 cup bread crumbs
2 eggs, beaten
1 teaspoon prepared mustard
2 tablespoons lemon juice
2 tablespoons canola oil

Flake salmon, reserving 1/3 cup of the liquid. Combine salmon with green onions, parsley and bread crumbs. Add eggs, mustard, lemon juice, and salmon liquid. Mix and form into patties. Fry in hot oil over medium heat until lightly browned on both sides. Drain on paper towels before serving.

TUNA TOFU PATTIES
Makes 4-6 Patties

1 can tuna, drained
1 block tofu, drained
1 egg, beaten
2 tablespoons chopped green onion
1/4 cup grated carrot
Salt, pepper, and soy sauce to taste

Mash tuna together with tofu in large bowl. Add egg, green onion, and grated carrot and season with salt, pepper, and soy sauce. Mix well and form into patties. Heat oil in pan and fry, turning patties over, until brown on both sides. Drain on absorbent paper before serving.

CHIVES WITH SARDINES
Serves 2

1 cup chopped chives
1 can (3.75 oz.) sardines packed in soybean oil
1 tablespoon soy sauce

Place chives over sardines; add soy sauce and let stand for about an hour. A great side dish served with rice.

TOFU CASSEROLE

1 block tofu, drained
1 can tuna, drained
1/2 can chopped chestnuts
1/2 cup chopped green onions
5 pieces shiitake, soaked, sliced
2 tablespoons shoyu
1 tablespoon sugar
1/2 teaspoon salt
1/2 pkg. dashi-no-moto
1/2 cup mayonnaise

Mix all ingredients together. Pour into 8 inch x 8 inch pan greased with oil from tuna. Bake at 350°F. for 35 to 45 minutes. (You may also add 1/2 can mushrooms chopped and/or 1/2 large carrot, grated).

VIOLET'S ZESTY BAKED SALMON   Serves 2-4

4 salmon filets (6-8 oz. each)

Zesty Sauce:
1/2 cup butter or mayonnaise
3 tablespoons soy sauce
2 tablespoons catsup
2 teaspoons powdered hot yellow mustard
1/2 teaspoon Worcestershire sauce
1 clove garlic, crushed

Arrange salmon filets in a lightly greased baking dish. Bake at 450°F. 15 minutes or until cooked through (the salmon should flake easily when tested with a fork). While salmon is baking, combine ingredients for Zesty Sauce and bring to a boil; simmer on low heat 5-10 minutes. Pour sauce over baked salmon and serve immediately.

Elaine Costello
Nuimono - Hawaii

FISH TIPS:

Fish is very fragile and cooks quickly so be careful to watch it closely as it cooks to prevent it from becoming dry and overcooked. As a fish cooks, its translucent flesh turns opaque; when it is opaque at the thickest part or slightly translucent at the center, you know it's done. Do not wait for the flesh to flake!

As a general guide, the total cooking time of any fish is estimated to be ten minutes for every inch of thickness, measured by the thickest part. This works for whole fish, steaks or fillets regardless of how it is cooked. Try it and you'll be amazed at the results!

These are some of our favorite flavors with fish:

Anise	Herbed vinegars
Basil	Lemon
Caraway seed	Lime
Chives	Orange
Chinese parsley (cilantro)	Parsley
Dill	Sage
Fennel	Tarragon
Garlic	Thyme
Ginger	

A typical Hawaiian luau consisted of lomi salmon, i'a maka (poke), opihi, wana, raw hee (octopus), raw crab (aama or kuhonu), chicken luau, chicken long rice, pipi kaula, sour poi, haupia and kulolo.

Notes

Soups & Stews

Salads

Salad Dressings

Soups, Stews
&
Salads

SOUPS & STEWS

BEEF CURRY STEW

Serves 6-8

>2 pounds stewing beef, cut into 1-inch cubes
>1/4 cup flour
>2 tablespoons canola oil
>2 large onions, wedged
>1 clove garlic, pressed
>1 quart water
>1/2 cup sherry
>2 teaspoons salt (add more as desired)
>1 tablespoon curry powder (add more as desired)
>1/2 teaspoon pepper
>4 carrots, cut into 1-inch pieces
>4 potatoes, quartered
>1 cup sliced celery
>1/4 cup flour
>1/4 cup water

Dredge beef in flour; brown lightly on all sides in hot oil.
Add onion and garlic; brown lightly. Add water; cover and
simmer 1 1/2 hours or until beef is tender. Add seasonings
and vegetables; cook additional 30 minutes or until vegetables are tender. Make paste of flour and water; add to
stew and cook until thickened.

CHICKEN MULLIGATAWNY SOUP

Serves 4-6

>1 stewing chicken, cut into bite-size pieces
>3 cups water
>1 sprig parsley, minced
>1/2 cup chopped celery
>1 medium carrot, diced
>1 medium potato, diced
>1 onion, sliced
>2 teaspoons curry powder
>1 1/2 teaspoons salt
>Dash of pepper

Simmer chicken in water for 1 1/2-2 hours or until tender. Cool slightly and remove meat from bones. Add remaining ingredients; heat to boiling. Cover and simmer 10 minutes or until vegetables are tender.

CORN CHOWDER
Serves 4-6

1/4 to 1/2 pound sliced bacon, cut into 1/2-inch strips
1 cup diced round onion
1 cup chopped celery
1 can (14.75 oz.) cream style corn
1 can (10.75 oz.) cream of potato soup
1 can (10.75 oz.) cream of mushroom or cream of
    chicken soup
1 cup water or 1 can (14 1/2 oz.) chicken broth
Paprika

Fry bacon until crisp. Drain, reserving 2 tablespoons of drippings in pan. Brown onions and celery in drippings until tender. Add cream style corn, soups, water and chicken broth. Stir until well blended. Simmer, uncovered, 5-10 minutes, stirring occasionally. Add bacon and garnish with paprika.

MOM'S EGG FLOWER SOUP
Makes 4 Cups

4 cups chicken broth
4 eggs, beaten until lemon colored
2 teaspoons soy sauce
Salt to taste
Chinese parsley or chopped green onions for garnish

Heat chicken broth until it comes to a boil. Add eggs, stirring constantly. Add soy sauce and salt to taste. To serve, garnish with parsley or onions.

HAWAIIAN STEW
Serves 6-8

"Olden Times" ono Hawaiian stew—a popular item on the dinner menu. Leftovers are also delicious for lunch and yes, even snacks!

2 tablespoons canola oil
1/4 pound salt pork, diced
12 small onions
2 pounds stewing beef, cubed
1 quart water
2 beef bouillon cubes, optional
2 teaspoons paprika, optional
1 teaspoon salt
Dash of pepper
3 medium tomatoes, cut into 1-inch cubes
4 medium carrots, pared and cut into 1-inch pieces
3 medium potatoes, pared and cut into 1-inch pieces
1 small head cabbage, wedged
Poi to thicken

Brown salt pork, onions and beef in hot oil. Add water, bouillon cubes, paprika, salt and pepper; stir until well blended; bring to a boil. Cover and simmer over low heat 1 1/2 hours. Add tomatoes, carrots and potatoes; simmer 30 minutes longer. Lay cabbage on top of stew; simmer additional 20 minutes or until tender. Remove cabbage and cut into bite-size pieces. Stir poi into stew until of desired thickness and serve stew topped with cabbage.

HEARTY BEAN SOUP
Serves 4-6

1 1/2 cups navy beans, washed and soaked overnight
2 quarts water
1 pound ham hocks
1 cup chopped onions
1/2 cup chopped celery
1 tablespoon chopped green pepper
1 tablespoon salt

1/2 teaspoon pepper
1/4 teaspoon thyme
2 bay leaves, broken

Drain beans and combine with remaining ingredients.
Bring to a boil; reduce heat to low and simmer 4-5 hours or
until beans are tender. Remove bones before serving.

HOT AND SOUR SOUP

Serves 4

4 cups chicken broth
2 ounces lean pork or chicken, cut into strips
2 tablespoons bamboo shoots, julienned
1 tablespoon tofu, julienned
1 tablespoon black fungus, softened in water and
    julienned
2 tablespoons soy sauce
1 teaspoon black pepper
3 tablespoons cornstarch
3 tablespoons water
2 eggs, beaten lightly
2 tablespoons vinegar
1 tablespoon sesame oil
1 teaspoon minced green onion

Combine chicken broth with pork or chicken, bamboo
shoots, tofu and black fungus. Bring to a boil. Add soy
sauce and pepper. Make paste of cornstarch and water;
add to soup, making certain that it is mixed in evenly. Add
eggs and vinegar to soup in a steady stream, stirring
slightly as you add. Add sesame oil and green onion just
before serving.

Robert Hsu, Owner/Manager
Maple Garden Restaurant

JHUK (Rice Soup)

Serves 6-8

Popo (grandmother) and Gun Gun (grandfather) knew how not to waste any food and Jhuk is a perfect example of how to prepare a nourishing and delicious soup with chicken or turkey bones. This recipe has been passed on for three generations, with some modifications, and is still being enjoyed by many today!

Chicken or turkey bones
3 quarts water
1 cup raw rice, washed and drained
4 pieces dried shiitake mushrooms, softened in water and
        slivered
1 1/2 teaspoons salt
1/2 teaspoon sherry
1/2 chung choi, minced
Minced green onion
Chinese parsley

In large pot, combine chicken or turkey bones and water; bring to boil and simmer 30 minutes. Remove bones and add rice, mushrooms, salt, sherry and chung choi; simmer additional 30-45 minutes. Garnish with green onion and Chinese parsley to serve.

MOCK BIRD'S NEST SOUP

Serves 12

2 bundles (1.4 oz. each) long rice
4 dried mushrooms, soaked until softened and finely
        chopped
6 cans (14.5 oz. each) chicken broth
1/4 teaspoon MSG, optional
1/2 pound ground pork
1/2 cup ham, finely chopped
1 can (8 oz.) water chestnuts, chopped
1/4 cup chopped Chinese parsley or green onions

Soak long rice in water for 30 minutes. When softened, cut

long rice into 1 1/2-inch lengths and set aside. In a pot, bring chicken broth to a boil. Add mushrooms, MSG, pork, ham and water chestnuts. Simmer for 30 minutes. Add long rice and simmer for another 15 minutes. Remove from heat; garnish with Chinese parsley or green onions. Serve hot.

KIM CHEE SOUP   Serves 4

1/4 lb. lean pork, cut into small pieces
1 teaspoon ginger, slivered
3 cups water
1 potato, pared and cut into bite size pieces
1 carrot, sliced
1/2 to 1 daikon or turnip, cut into strips
Green onion, chopped (amount according to taste)
1/2 to 1 cup kim chee, chopped
1-2 tablespoons red miso

Stir fry pork and ginger in a non-stick sauce pan. Add water to pan and bring to a boil; simmer for 2-3 minutes. Add potato, carrots, daikon, and green onion. Simmer until vegetables are tender, approximately 8-10 minutes. Add kim chee and miso; simmer for additional 1-2 minutes.

Donna Y. Shiraki Hashimoto
MCC Board

Moiliili Triangle Mini Park, located across the street from the Moiliili Community Center, was the original site of Kashiwabara's Japanese Language School.

LEAN PORTUGUESE BEAN SOUP

1-2 ham hocks
Water
1/2 pound Portuguese sausage, sliced
1 onion, chopped
3 carrots, sliced
2 stalks celery, chopped
1 salad potato, optional
1 small cabbage
1 clove garlic
1/8 cup green pepper, minced
1 can (8 oz.) tomato sauce
2 peppercorns
1 teaspoon minced parsley, optional
1/8 teaspoon mustard
1 bay leaf
Salt and pepper to taste
1 can (14.5 oz.) red kidney beans
1 cup cooked macaroni

Cover ham hocks with water and boil 10 minutes. Drain and replace with fresh water; bring to boil again and simmer for 2 hours or until meat falls from the bone. In last half hour or so, add Portuguese sausage. Remove from heat and allow to cool; drain and refrigerate stock overnight. Remove meat from bones and shred; refrigerate. The next day, skim fat off top of stock. Add shredded ham and sausage and all other ingredients except kidney beans and macaroni. Cook until vegetables are tender. Add kidney beans and simmer for 1/2 hour. Add cooked macaroni to individual bowls before serving soup.

Note: Goes great with Portuguese sweet bread.

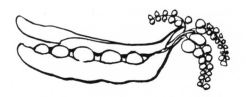

OLD FASHIONED BEEF STEW
Serves 6-8

2 pounds lean stewing beef, cut into 1-inch cubes
1/2 cup flour
1/4 cup canola oil
2 medium onions, wedged
1 clove garlic, pressed
5 cups water
2 bay leaves, broken
1/2 cup sherry
2 teaspoons salt (add more as desired)
1/4 teaspoon pepper
2 can (8 oz.) tomato sauce
1 can (13.5 oz.) whole tomatoes
4 carrots, cubed
4 potatoes, pared and quartered
1 cup sliced celery

Dredge beef in flour; brown lightly on all sides in hot oil. Add onions and garlic; brown lightly. Add water and bay leaves; simmer 1 1/2 hours or until beef is tender. Add remaining ingredients; simmer additional 30 minutes or until vegetables are tender. If desired, stew may be thickened with flour-water mixture.

PORTUGUESE BEAN SOUP
Serves 8-10

2 ham shanks
1 package (12 oz.) Portuguese sausage, cut into 1/2-inch
      pieces
1 quart water
1 can (8 oz.) tomato sauce
1 large onion, wedged
2 potatoes, cubed
1 carrot, cubed
1 1/2 teaspoons salt
Dash of pepper
2 cans (15 oz. size) kidney beans

Simmer ham shanks and Portuguese sausage in water for 2 hours; add more water if needed. Add remaining ingredients; cook 15 minutes or until vegetables are tender. Serve hot.

SALADS

AVOCADO GELATIN   Serves 9-12

> 1 package unflavored gelatin
> 1/2 cup cold water
> 1 box (6 oz.) lime flavored gelatin
> 1/2 cup sugar
> 1 cup hot water
> 1 cup avocado, pureed
> 1/2 cup milk
> 1/2 cup mayonnaise

Dissolve gelatin in cold water. To lime flavored gelatin, add sugar, hot water and softened gelatin; stir until dissolved. In a separate bowl, mix together avocado puree, milk, and mayonnaise. Combine all ingredients, mixing well. Pour into 8 x 8-inch pan. Chill until set, about 4 hours.

BAVARIAN SAUSAGE SALAD   Serves 4

> 3 tablespoons vinegar
> 1 tablespoon dijon or dark mustard
> 2 tablespoons vegetable oil
> 1/2 teaspoon salt
> 1/4 teaspoon pepper
> 1/4 teaspoon paprika
> 1/4 teaspoon sugar
> 1 tablespoon capers
> 1/2 pound knockwurst, cooked and cut into small cubes
> 2 small dill pickles, minced
> 1 onion, minced
> 1 tablespoon parsley, chopped

Mix together vinegar, mustard and oil. Add salt, pepper, paprika and sugar. Adjust amount of seasonings as desired. Add capers; mix well. Stir in knockwurst, pickles and onions. Garnish with parsley just before serving.

CHICKEN CUCUMBER

Serves 4

1 pound cooked chicken breast, shredded
1 cucumber, sliced

Sauce:
1 clove garlic
1 slice ginger
1 tablespoon vinegar
3 tablespoons soy sauce
1 tablespoon sugar
1/2 teaspoon sesame seeds, toasted
2 tablespoon sesame seed oil
Dash MSG to taste, optional

Combine ingredients for Sauce. Let stand 1 hour or longer. Before serving, mix chicken and cucumber and toss with sauce. **Note:** Double recipe for sauce if more desired.

HOT CRAB POTATO SALAD

Serves 8

1 large potato, cooked and cut into 1-inch cubes
1 hard-cooked egg, chopped
1/2 cup celery, chopped
1 cup mayonnaise
1 cup cabbage, chopped
1/2 cup round onion, minced
1 can (8 oz.) water chestnuts, chopped
1 pound shrimp, shelled and cleaned
1/2 cup imitation crab, shredded
1 block (7 oz.) kamaboko, slivered
Bread or cracker crumbs

Mix together all ingredients, except bread or cracker crumbs. Spread evenly in nonstick 10-inch or larger square pan. Top with bread or cracker crumbs. Bake at 350°F. 40-45 minutes or until crust is browned. **Note:** For variation, substitute one egg, scrambled for hard cooked. Sprinkle scrambled egg on top; bake, uncovered.

CHICKEN SALAD

Serves 25-30

3 pounds chicken breast
2 tablespoons soy sauce
1 tablespoon hoisin sauce
1 teaspoon salt
6 stalks green onion, chopped
1 bunch parsley, chopped
1 1/2 cups preserved ginger
2 medium heads lettuce, shredded
1 cup mixed nuts, chopped
1 bottle (2 1/2 oz.) sesame seeds, toasted

Dressing:
9 tablespoons white vinegar
3/4 cup sesame oil
6 tablespoons sugar
3 teaspoons salt
1/4 teaspoon pepper
1 tablespoon MSG, optional

Marinate chicken in soy sauce, salt, and hoisin sauce for 15 minutes. Bake at 350°F. for 20-30 minutes or until cooked. Shred chicken into long strips. Add green onion, parsley and preserved ginger. Mix in shredded lettuce, nuts and sesame seeds. Combine Dressing ingredients and toss with salad just before serving.

Raelene Chock
Principal
Kaimuki High School

Ala Naio Stream runs across the street from the now closed Willows Restaurant where, at one time, a large duck pond, a favorite swimming hole for the whole community, was located at the curve.

CHINESE-STYLE CHICKEN SALAD　　Serves 8-10

Chicken salad is everyone's favorite. It is adaptable and can be served on dozens of occasions. It can be dressed down and taken on a picnic or dressed up and served at a dinner party.

1 medium head lettuce, shredded
1/2 cup minced green onion
1 bunch Chinese parsley (cilantro), chopped
1/4 cup thinly sliced celery, optional
1 package (3 oz.) fried won ton strips
1/4 cup chopped roast peanuts
1 pound cooked boneless chicken breast, shredded
1/2 cup char siu, julienned

Sesame Vinegar Dressing:
2 tablespoons toasted sesame seeds
1 teaspoon salt
1/2 teaspoon pepper
1/4 cup sugar
1/3 cup rice vinegar
1/4 cup salad oil

Combine lettuce, onion, Chinese parsley and celery in a large salad bowl; toss to mix well. Sprinkle with won ton strips, peanuts, chicken and char siu.

Combine ingredients for Sesame Vinegar Dressing; mix well and pour over salad just before serving.

Variation:
Chinese Crab Salad: Substitute 1 cup cooked crab meat for chicken.

Moiliili Field was once the site for community activities such as bazaars and circuses as well as for the baseball games for which it is known today.

CLASSIC POTATO
MACARONI SALAD

Whenever there is a family gathering, everyone asks for this salad...its simple flavor is palatable to all and goes well with anything that is served!

3 cups cooked elbow macaroni, drained and chilled
3 cups cooked salad or new potatoes, cubed and chilled
1/2 cup minced onion
1 cup cooked frozen peas and carrots, drained and chilled
1/4 cup minced celery, optional
3 tablespoons sweet pickle relish, optional
1/2 cup cooked shrimp or crab meat
4 hard-cooked eggs, diced
1 teaspoon salt (add more as desired)
1/2 teaspoon white pepper
3 cups mayonnaise (add more as desired)
Paprika

Combine all ingredients, except mayonnaise; toss gently to mix well. Add mayonnaise and mix thoroughly. Sprinkle lightly with paprika and garnish as desired.

CRANBERRY RELISH MOLD

2 packages (3 oz. each) cherry gelatin
1 teaspoon unflavored gelatin
2 cups boiling water
1 can (16 oz.) whole cranberry sauce
1 can (7 oz.) crushed pineapple, drained
1/4 cup chopped celery

Dissolve cherry and unflavored gelatins completely in boiling water. Let cool slightly and stir in cranberry sauce, pineapple and celery. Pour into glass serving bowl or 6-oz. mold. Chill until firm, about 3-4 hours.

GERMAN POTATO SALAD

Serves 8-12

3/4 pounds bacon
1 onion, chopped
2 tablespoons flour
3/4 cup white vinegar
2 cups water
1/2 teaspoon salt
1 teaspoon sugar
1/4 teaspoon pepper
5 pounds red potatoes, cooked with skin on
2 teaspoons salt
5 stalks celery, chopped

Fry bacon and chop into small pieces. Add onions to bacon fat and sauté; remove onions from fat and drain 2/3 of fat from pan. Do not turn heat off. Add flour to fat and mix; add vinegar, water, salt, sugar and pepper; cook until clear.

Peel potatoes and cut into slices while still hot; sprinkle with salt and add celery, onion, bacon and bacon sauce. Mix well and let stand several hours to let flavors blend. Serve at room temperature.

At one time, the area between Kuni Island Fabrics and Kinko's was once the site for the German Consulate and it was known as "German Town."

POTATO-MACARONI SALAD

Serves 10-12

4 or 5 cooked new potatoes, cut into 1-inch cubes
3 cups cooked macaroni, drained well
1 package (1 pound) imitation crab, shredded
1 package (1 pound) frozen peas
1 medium round onion, chopped
1 small apple, chopped
2 tomatoes, seeded and chopped
2 tablespoons sweet relish, drained
4 or 5 hard-cooked eggs, chopped
Assorted chopped olives, optional
Salt and pepper to taste
MSG to taste, optional
1 cup mayonnaise (more if needed)

Mix all ingredients together in a large salad bowl. Add enough mayonnaise to moisten; mix well.

MARINATED CRUNCHY SALAD

Serves 6-8

1 can cut green beans, drained
1 can petite peas, drained
1 can shoepeg corn, drained
1 1/2 teaspoons salt
1/2 cup chopped onion
1 jar (4 oz.) diced pimento
1 cup sugar
1 cup vinegar
1/4 cup salad oil

Combine beans, peas and corn into a mixing bowl and sprinkle with salt; refrigerate 1 hour. Drain any liquid and add onion and pimento.

Heat sugar, vinegar and oil in saucepan until sugar dissolves. Pour over vegetables and chill overnight.

Senator Matt Matsunaga

SOMEN SALAD

Serves 6-8

1 package (9 oz.) somen
1/3 cup sugar
1 cup dashi or chicken broth
1/3 cup soy sauce
1/3 cup rice vinegar
1 tablespoon sesame oil
3 cups shredded head lettuce
1/2 block (7 oz.) kamaboko, slivered
1/4 pound char siu, slivered
1 small cucumber, slivered
1/4 cup minced green onion
1 sheet nori, cut into strips
Fried egg strips

Cook somen according to package directions; rinse, drain and chill. To prepare sauce, combine sugar, broth, soy sauce, rice vinegar and sesame oil in saucepan; bring to a boil then simmer 3-4 minutes over low heat. Chill.

To serve, arrange cold somen on bed of shredded lettuce; garnish with remaining ingredients and pour chilled sauce over just before serving.

Hawaiian Royalty enjoyed swimming in the waters of Kapaakea Springs, the present site of the now closed Willows Restaurant, which were believed to have had healing powers.

ST. LOUIS SUNSET SALAD

Serves 4-6

1 bunch watercress, washed and cleaned
1 medium papaya
1 medium red pepper
1 bottle (8 oz.) Maui onion dressing
Fresh ground black pepper

Break off long stems of watercress and discard. Break small stems into 2-inch lengths. Place leaves and small stems in a salad bowl. Peel papaya and scoop out seeds; slice papaya into 2-inch strips and combine with watercress in salad bowl. Wash and slice red pepper into narrow lengthwise strips. Combine with watercress and papaya. Toss with Maui onion dressing and black pepper as desired.

Rebecca Ryan
Executive Director
Moiliili Community Center

TOFU SALAD

Serves 8

1 block firm tofu, drained and cubed
1 can (16 oz.) salmon, drained and flaked
1 large tomato, diced
1 small onion, chopped
1 package (12 oz.) bean sprouts
1 bunch watercress, cut into 1 1/2 inch pieces
1/2 cup green onion, chopped

Dressing:
1/2 cup light salad oil
3 cloves garlic, minced
1/4 cup soy sauce

On a large platter, spread ingredients in layers in the following order: tofu, salmon, tomato, onion, bean sprouts, watercress, and 1/4 cup of the green onion.

To make Dressing, combine salad oil and garlic in a saucepan and bring to a boil. Remove from heat; add soy sauce and remaining green onion. Mix well. Pour the prepared dressing over the salad and serve immediately.

Mazie K. Hirono
Lieutenant Governor
State of Hawaii

SALAD TIPS

• Balance textures - crunchy with soft, cooked with raw, succulent with crisp.

• Salads that are served with a meal should complement it — a heavy meal requires a light salad and a light entree, a heartier salad.

• Add just enough dressing to coat the salad lightly and add the dressing at the last minute to prevent the greens from wilting.

• All ingredients should be of the best quality...oil and vinegars should be the best you can afford. Vegetables and fruits must be fresh and ripe and cooked ingredients should be done "just right."

• Mix chilled leftover cooked vegetables with bottled salad dressings for a last minute salad.

SERVING SALAD GREENS

• Use a variety of greens for interesting textures, flavors and colors. Add fresh herbs for a special touch!

• Prepare the greens by washing each leaf with cool water; drain and store in plastic bag in the refrigerator. The greens should be completely drip-dried before tossing with your favorite dressing.

SALAD DRESSINGS

FAVORITE FRENCH DRESSING   Makes 1 1/2 Cups

1/4 cup brown or white sugar
1/2 teaspoon dry mustard
1/8 teaspoon pepper
1/4 teaspoon celery salt, optional
1/2 teaspoon salt
1/2 teaspoon Worcestershire sauce
1/2 cup tomato catsup
3/4 cup canola oil
1/4 cup cider or rice vinegar
1/4 cup minced onion

Combine ingredients in a jar. Cover and refrigerate. Shake well before using.

ORIENTAL DRESSING   Makes 1 Cup

1/3 cup rice vinegar
1/4 cup canola oil
1/4 cup soy sauce
1/4 cup sugar
1 tablespoon dry sherry, optional
1 tablespoon toasted sesame seeds, optional
1 teaspoon grated fresh ginger or 1/4 teaspoon ground
      ginger
1 drop sesame oil, optional

Combine all ingredients in a jar; cover tightly and shake to mix well. Serve over greens.

> *The major modes of transportation for residents of Moiliili at one time included street cars, horse-and-buggies and bicycles.*

POPPY SEED DRESSING
Makes 4 Cups

1 1/4 cups sugar
2 teaspoons dry mustard
2 teaspoons salt
3 tablespoons onion juice
2/3 cup cider or rice vinegar
2 cups canola oil
3 tablespoons poppy seeds

Combine all ingredients in a jar. Cover and store in refrigerator. Shake well before using over greens.

SALAD DRESSING
Makes About 1 1/4 Cups

1/2 cup vinegar
1/2 cup sugar
1/2 teaspoon salt
Pepper to taste
1/4 cup water
1 teaspoon (or more as desired) Italian salad dressing
8 pieces dried shrimp

Combine vinegar, sugar, salt, pepper and water in a sauce pan. Heat until sugar dissolves; cool. Once cooled, pour into jar and add Italian dressing (do not use ranch-style dressing). Cover and shake well. Add shrimp and let stand overnight before serving.

THOUSAND ISLAND DRESSING
Makes 1 1/4 Cups

1 cup mayonnaise
2 tablespoons chili sauce
1 tablespoon sweet pickle relish, drained
1 tablespoon chopped green bell pepper, optional
1 hard-cooked egg, chopped

Combine ingredients; mix well and chill.

WAIOLI GUAVA DRESSING

Makes 3 1/4 Cups

1 cup mayonnaise
1 cup catsup
1/4 cup vinegar
1/2 cup salad oil
1 teaspoon dry mustard
2 teaspoons lemon juice
1/2 cup guava jelly or jam
1/2 teaspoon garlic salt

Combine all ingredients in blender and blend or beat with rotary beater until well blended. Chill and serve over your favorite tossed salad.

The Original Waioli Tea Room Restaurant

Vegetables

Vegetables

VEGETABLES

ARAIMO AND KONNYAKU NO ITAME MONO
(Simmered Dasheen Potatoes with Tuber Root Cake)   Serves 4-6

> 1 pound chicken wings, tips removed and cut in half
> 1 tablespoon salad oil
> 1 pound araimo, peeled and cut into bite size pieces
> 1/2 cup boiling water
> 2 konnyaku, cut into bite size pieces
> 2 tablespoons sugar
> 1/2 cup soy sauce
> 1 tablespoon mirin
> 1/2 pound string beans, parboiled with a pinch of salt

Brown chicken in hot oil for 2-3 minutes. Add araimo; mix slowly and cook 2-3 minutes. Add Konnyaku and water, mixing slowly with rice paddle; cook 10 minutes on medium heat. Add sugar and 1/4 cup soy sauce; cook for additional 10 minutes. Add string beans, remaining soy sauce and mirin; simmer another 3-4 minutes or until araimo is cooked.

AUNTY PAT'S
SENGIRI DAIKON SANBAIZUKE   Makes About 1 Quart

> 1 package (3 oz.) sengiri daikon
> 1 package (3 oz.) kiri konbu
>
> Sauce:
> 1/2 cup rice vinegar
> 1 cup sugar
> 1/2 cup soy sauce
> Grated fresh ginger and chili pepper to taste

Soak daikon and konbu in warm water for about 1 hour; rinse, drain and squeeze dry. Combine Sauce ingredients in large bowl; mix well and add daikon and konbu. Let stand 2-3 days in covered jar in refrigerator before serving.

Elaine Costello
Nuimono - Hawaii

BAKED BEANS NO. 1

Serves 12-15

- **1 cup bacon, chopped**
- **1/2 cup Portuguese sausage, chopped**
- **1 pound ground beef**
- **1 medium onion, chopped**
- **1 large can (53 oz.) and 1 small can (28 oz.) baked beans**
- **1 can (14.5 oz) red kidney beans, drained and rinsed**
- **1 can (14.5 oz.) garbanzo beans, drained and rinsed, optional**
- **1 cup grated cheddar cheese**
- **1 cup brown sugar, packed**
- **3/4 cup catsup**
- **1 teaspoon dry mustard**
- **1 teaspoon Worcestershire sauce**

Brown bacon and Portuguese sausage. Add beef and onion and fry. Mix all ingredients together in an oven safe dish; bake at 350°F. 45 minutes. Serve warm.

Note: This recipe is on the sweet side. If you prefer, you can cut down on the sugar or add more catsup. This recipe goes well with baked ham.

Senator and Mrs. Brian Taniguchi

BAKED BEANS NO. 2

1 medium onion, chopped well
7 slices turkey bacon, sliced in 1/4-inch strips
1 package turkey hot dogs, sliced
1 can (28 oz.) baked beans
1 teaspoon sugar, optional

Pan fry onions, bacon and hot dogs in skillet until onions are translucent and hot dogs and bacon are cooked. Add baked beans and sugar; simmer for 5-10 minutes. Serve over hot rice.

CABBAGE MISOZUKE

2 pounds head cabbage
1/2 cup miso
1/2 cup sugar
1/4 cup vinegar
1 tablespoon salt

Chop the cabbage into chunks. Mix the remaining ingredients. Pour over the cabbage and mix well. Let stand 3-4 hours before serving.

Note: If made after lunch, it will be ready to serve at supper.

CUCUMBER PICKLES

8 cucumbers

Solution:
2 cups sugar
1 cup vinegar
1/2 cup Hawaiian salt
Chili pepper or pepper sauce to taste, optional

Cut cucumbers in chunks or lengthwise. Place in a gallon

jar. Combine solution ingredients; mix well and pour over cucumbers. Leave in refrigerator.

Note: You may make 1/4 recipe of solution for 3 cucumbers.

DAIKON EGGPLANT
Serves 4-6

> 4 to 5 long eggplant, sliced in quarters lengthwise, then cut into 2-3" lengths
> 1/2 cup water
> 1/2 cup prepared soba dashi (tsuyu)
> 2 tablespoons green onions, chopped
> 2 teaspoons ground sesame seeds
> 1/2 cup bonito flakes (katsuo)
> 1 daikon, grated

Steam eggplant until tender (or microwave in covered dish about 4 minutes). Heat wok or frying pan and spray with non-stick cooking spray or use 1 teaspoon sesame oil. Stir fry eggplant for 1 to 2 minutes. Add water and one-half of the dashi; cover and cook until eggplant is soft. Place eggplant in a deep dish; cover with green onions, sesame seeds and bonito flakes. Squeeze out liquid from daikon and place daikon over top of eggplant. Pour remaining dashi over daikon and eggplant.

MASHED POTATOES
Serves 2-3

> 2 potatoes, peeled and cubed
> 1 can (14.5 oz.) chicken broth

Place potatoes in a saucepan and cover with chicken broth; bring to a boil and cook until done. When potatoes are cooked, drain and set aside liquid. Mash potatoes. If potatoes are too dry, add broth.

DAIKON SANBAIZUKE (Pickled Turnip) Makes About 2 Quarts

> 5 pounds daikon or turnip
> 1/2 package kirikonbu
> 2 cups sugar
> 1 cup soy sauce
> 1/3 cup rice vinegar
> 1 teaspoon grated fresh ginger
> 2 chili peppers, seeded and minced

Clean and peel daikon. Wash kirikonbu and squeeze out excess water. Mix remaining ingredients together and pour over daikon and kirikonbu. Put into a quart jar; cover and refrigerate.

GERMAN POTATO PANCAKES Serves 4

> 6 large potatoes, mashed
> 2 eggs, beaten
> 1 1/2 tablespoons flour
> 1/4 teaspoon baking powder
> 1 1/2 teaspoons salt
> 1 onion, grated

Mix all ingredients. Drop by spoonfuls into pan with 1/4 inch hot cooking oil; brown on both sides. Drain on absorbent paper. Delicious when served with applesauce.

EGGPLANT WITH
HOT GARLIC SAUCE Serves 4

> Sauce:
> 1 teaspoon minced ginger
> 1 teaspoon minced garlic
> 1 1/2 tablespoons soy sauce
> 1 teaspoon sugar
> 1 teaspoon white vinegar

1 teaspoon minced fresh red chili pepper or
1/4 teaspoon dried chili pepper flakes
1 teaspoon cornstarch

1 pound eggplant, pared and cut into 1-inch strips
1/4 cup pork, cut into strips
1 cup vegetable oil

Mix Sauce ingredients in a small mixing bowl; set aside. Heat oil in skillet or wok; add eggplant and fry until pulp is brown but not burnt. Remove eggplant from oil using sieve; drain excess oil. Stir-fry pork in 1 tablespoon hot oil over high heat 1 minute or until cooked; drain pork and pour oil out. Heat Sauce in pan until near boiling; add eggplant and pork. Toss together gently and cook until Sauce comes to a boil.

Robert Hsu, Owner/Manager
Maple Garden Restaurant

PICKLED LAHAINA NASUBI   Makes About 1 1/2 Quarts

4-5 pounds Lahaina nasubi
1/2 cup Hawaiian salt
1 cup sugar
3 cups water
1/3 cup Japanese rice vinegar
1 can beer

Mix together salt, sugar, water, vinegar and beer; add to nasubi. Place weight on for 1 1/2 - 2 days at room temperature. Refrigerate.

Elaine Costello
Nuimono - Hawaii

JAPANESE-STYLE
COOKED PUMPKIN

Serves 6

1/2 medium pumpkin, seeded
2 tablespoons vegetable oil
1 1/2 to 2 cups water
2 tablespoons sugar
1/2 package (.225 oz.) Dashi-no-moto (powdered soup
   base)
1 tablespoons soy sauce
1 teaspoon mirin
1 tablespoon sake

Cut pumpkin into 2 inch cubes and trim off skin. Heat oil in deep skillet or Dutch oven. Cook pumpkin in oil for approximately 1 minute on high heat, stirring quickly to prevent burning and sticking. Add water, sugar and Dashi-no-moto. Cover and cook until pumpkin is tender. Combine soy sauce, mirin and sake and add to the pumpkin. Stir to coat pumpkin. Cover and cook for 15 minutes on low heat. Turn heat off and let stand in pot for another 15 minutes to improve flavor before serving.

KINPIRA GOBO (Sautéed Burdock)

Serves 4

1 good-sized gobo, scraped and cut into 2-inch long
      matchsticks
Water to cover burdock
1 teaspoon Japanese rice vinegar
1 carrot, pared and cut into 2-inch long matchsticks
1 1/2 tablespoon sesame seed oil
1 tablespoon sugar
1/2 tablespoon mirin or sherry
1 tablespoon soy sauce
1/4 cup water
1 dried chili pepper, seeded and minced
1 tablespoon toasted sesame seeds

Soak gobo in water to cover and vinegar for 15-20 minutes; drain. Pat dry on towel before use. Sauté gobo and carrot sticks in sesame oil over high heat. Add sugar, mirin or sherry, soy sauce and water. Simmer on low heat until liquid is absorbed. Add chili pepper and sesame seeds. Serve hot over steamed rice.

ODEN (Vegetables Simmered in Stock)   Serves 6-8

10 araimo (dasheen)
1 chikuwa
1 kamaboko
2 konnyaku
2 large daikon
1 can (8.5 oz.) bamboo shoots

Stock:
3 cups water
1 packet dashi-no-moto
5 tablespoons soy sauce
1/4 cup sugar
I teaspoon salt

Parboil araimo and remove skin. Cut chikuwa, kamaboko, konnyaku, daikon and bamboo shoots into large chunks. In a large pot, prepare stock by combining water, dashi-no-moto, soy sauce, sugar, and salt; bring to a boil. Add all ingredients, lower heat to low and simmer for about 50 minutes or until vegetables are tender.

PICKLED MUSTARD
EGGPLANT

Makes about 1 Quart

2 teaspoons dry yellow mustard
1/2 cup sugar
1/2 cup vinegar
1/2 cup soy sauce
1/2 teaspoon MSG, optional
5-6 long eggplant, sliced

Mix together mustard, sugar, vinegar, soy sauce, and MSG.
Pour sauce over eggplant and soak. Refrigerator 4-5 days.

ROLLER'S CUKE

Serves About 20-24

5 pounds cucumber
1/4 cup sugar

1 cup soy sauce
1 cup sugar
1-1/2 teaspoons salt
1/4 cup apple cider vinegar
Chili pepper (optional)

Slice cucumbers and sprinkle with 1/4 cup sugar. Allow to
stand for 3 hours, then drain. Combine remaining ingredients in a saucepan and bring mixture to a boil; pour hot
mixture over drained cucumbers; cool. Keep refrigerated.

Note: Stays crispy!

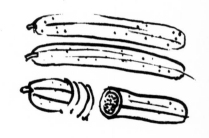

SCALLOPED POTATOES   **Serves 4-6**

"Hi Gang! This is such a good dish! A perfect compliment for your Sunday dinners...goes along great with ribs, roasts or steaks."

8 slices bacon, cut into 1/2-inch pieces
1 medium round onion, minced
4 large gem potatoes
1 can (10.75 oz.) cream of mushroom soup
1 cup whole milk
Sliced American cheese, cut into strips
Paprika

Brown bacon and onions in saucepan; set aside. Peel potatoes then cut in lengthwise halves and cut into 1/8-inch thick slices.

Place potatoes in a lightly greased casserole dish or disposable baking pan (I prefer this because I hate to scrub off burnt cheese). Mix in bacon-onion mixture, mushroom soup and milk; mix well. Place cheese strips all over the top of potatoes and sprinkle with paprika for color. Bake at 375°F. 1 hour.

Hari Kojima, TV2 Host
Hari's Kitchen and
Let's Go Fishing

STUFFED ROUND EGGPLANT

Serves 3-4

6- 8 small round eggplant

Filling:
1/2 pound lean ground beef
1 teaspoon oyster sauce
1 teaspoon salt
4 dried shiitake mushrooms, soaked in water to soften and minced
1/4 cup minced green onion
1 small can (8 oz.) water chestnuts, chopped fine
2 eggs, beaten

1/2 cup flour for dredging
1/2-3/4 cup panko or bread crumbs
1 quart oil for frying

Lemon Shoyu Sauce:
1/4 cup soy sauce
1/4 teaspoon lemon juice
1 teaspoon dry wine
1/4 teaspoon fresh ginger juice

Cut eggplant into lengthwise halves to form a "pocket" but do not cut through; set aside. Combine ground beef, oyster sauce, salt, mushrooms, onion, water chestnuts and 1 egg and mix well. Fill the pocket or space between eggplant slices with mixture; you may need wooden picks or small skewers to hold opening closed. Roll eggplant in flour, dip in remaining egg, then roll in panko or bread crumbs. Deep fry in hot oil until brown on both sides. Drain on absorbent paper and serve with Lemon-Shoyu Sauce made by combining all ingredients listed above.

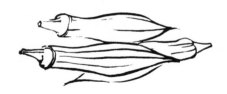

Notes

Cakes

Cookies

Pies

Sweets
Cakes, Cookies, Pies & Desserts
Desserts

CAKES

BANANA PUDDING CAKE   Serves 8-10

1 box (18.5 oz.) yellow cake mix
1 small box (3.5 oz.) instant vanilla pudding
4 eggs
1 cup water
1/2 cup ripe mashed bananas
1/4 cup oil

Mix all ingredients together and pour into a greased tube pan. Bake at 350°F. 45-55 minutes or until done.

BLUEBERRY CREAM CAKE   Serves 20-24

Crust:
1 1/2 blocks butter
1 1/2 cups flour
1/4 cup brown sugar, packed
1/2 cup chopped nuts

Filling:
1 box (3 oz.) lemon flavored gelatin
1 cup hot water
3/4 cup sugar
1 package (8 oz.) cream cheese, softened
1/2 pint whipping cream, whipped

1 can blueberry pie filling

To prepare Crust, cream sugar and butter; add flour and nuts and mix to blend together. Press into 9 x 13-inch pan. Bake at 350°F. 10-15 minutes or until crust is lightly browned.

Prepare Filling by dissolving gelatin in hot water; cool. Cream sugar and cream cheese. Add gelatin mixture to cream cheese mixture; fold in whipped cream. Pour into baked crust and refrigerate until set, about 2-3 hours. Top with canned blueberries when ready to serve.

BUTTER CAKE WITH
COCONUT FROSTING

Serves 8-10

1 cup butter
2 cups sugar
5 large eggs
3 cups cake flour
4 1/2 teaspoons baking powder
Pinch of salt
1 cup milk
1 teaspoon lemon extract
1 teaspoon vanilla extract

Filling:
1 box (4 oz.) lemon pie filling

Frosting:
2 egg whites
1 cup white corn syrup
Pinch of salt
1 teaspoon vanilla
1 cup grated fresh coconut

Cream butter; add sugar gradually and beat until light and fluffy. Add eggs, one at a time, beating well after each addition. Sift dry ingredients together and add alternately to creamed mixture with milk, starting and ending with dry mixture. Add extracts and pour into buttered 10 x 15-inch pan. Bake at 350°F. 40 minutes or until done. Cool. Fill with 1 box (4 oz.) lemon pie filling prepared according to box directions.

To prepare Frosting, beat egg whites until frothy. Heat corn syrup and salt until mixture begins to boil. Slowly add hot syrup to beaten egg whites, beating constantly until stiff and of spreading consistency; add vanilla. Frost cake and sprinkle coconut on top.

Mrs. Maggie Inouye
Wife of U.S. Senator Daniel K. Inouye

CHOCOLATE CAKE

Serves 10-12

1 box (18.25 oz.) pudding chocolate cake mix
1 cup mayonnaise
1 cup water
3 eggs

Frosting:
1 can (16 oz.) prepared cake frosting

Grease and flour two 9-inch layer cake pans; set aside. To prepare cake, combine cake mix, mayonnaise, water and eggs in large mixer bowl; mix at low speed for 30 seconds; then beat at medium speed for 2 minutes or 300 strokes by hand. Pour into prepared pans. Bake at 350°°F. 30-35 minutes or until cake pulls away from sides of pan and center springs back when touched lightly. Cool in pan for 10 minutes; remove and let cool on wire rack. Frost after cake has cooled completely.

CRAZY CAKE

Serves 20-24

Cake:
5 tablespoons cocoa powder
3 cups sifted flour
2 cups sugar
1 teaspoon salt
2 teaspoons baking soda
1 teaspoon vanilla
2 tablespoons vinegar
2/3 cup canola oil
2/3 cup water

Frosting:
1/2 cup margarine or butter
3/4 cup sugar
1/4 cup evaporated milk
2/3 cup chocolate chips
1/2 cup chopped nuts

To prepare Cake, mix the dry ingredients in a bowl by hand. Make a well in the center and add the vanilla, vinegar and oil; mix with a fork until dry ingredients are moistened. Pour water over and stir until well-mixed. Bake in ungreased 9 x 13-inch pan at 350°F. 20-30 minutes or until done.

To prepare Frosting, combine margarine or butter, sugar and milk; bring to a boil and remove from heat. Add chocolate chips; stir until smooth. Add nuts and mix well. Frost cake while still warm.

JOE DIFFIE'S CAKE

Serves 9-12

2 cups flour
2 eggs
1 teaspoon baking soda
1 cup grated coconut
1 can (8 oz.) undrained crushed pineapple

Sauce:
1 cup sugar
1 cup milk
1/2 cup butter

To prepare cake, combine flour, eggs, baking soda, coconut and crushed pineapple; mix well. Pour into greased 9 x 9-inch pan and bake at 350°F. 45-50 minutes or until inserted toothpick comes out clean.

To make Sauce, combine all ingredients and simmer over low heat for 5 minutes, stirring occasionally. Pour over cake.

CREAMY CHEESECAKE

Serves 8-10

Crust:
1 1/2 cups chocolate wafer crumbs
1/4 cup brown sugar, packed
1/3 cup butter, melted

Filling:
1 package (8 oz.) cream cheese
1 can (15 oz.) sweetened condensed milk
1/3 cup lemon juice
1 cup whipping cream

Topping:
Fresh or canned fruits

In a small bowl, blend together chocolate wafer crumbs and brown sugar. Mix in melted butter. Press crumb mixture onto sides and bottom of 9-inch springform cake pan or 9-inch pie dish. Bake at 375°F. 8-10 minutes. Remove and set aside to cool.

In a large mixing bowl, beat cream cheese until light and fluffy. Beat in condensed milk and lemon juice. In a separate bowl, beat whipping cream until stiff. Fold whipped cream into cream cheese mixture until well blended. Spread over cooled crust and refrigerate 2-3 hours or until set. Top with fruits before serving.

Representative Terry Nui Yoshinaga

There was a time when there used to be a cave located about 100 yards across from the Varsity Theater where Hans Kashiwabara used to fish for mullets.

MANDARIN ORANGE CAKE

Serves 20-24

1 box (18.5 oz.) yellow cake mix
1/2 cup canola oil
4 eggs
1 can mandarin oranges, undrained

Topping:
1 can (8 oz.) crushed pineapple with syrup
1 box (3.5 oz.) instant vanilla pudding mix
1 container (8 oz.) non-dairy whipped topping
Coconut flakes or mandarin oranges, optional

To prepare cake, combine cake mix, oil, eggs, and undrained mandarin oranges, using electric mixer. Beat 4 minutes on medium speed. Pour mixture into greased and floured 13 x 9 x 2-inch pan and bake at 350°F. 35-45 minutes or until inserted toothpick comes out clean. Remove from oven and allow to cool.

To make Topping, combine undrained pineapple and pudding mix; mix well. Fold in whipped topping. Spread evenly over cooled cake. If desired, sprinkle coconut flakes or arrange can of drained mandarin oranges on top.

Kuilei Street and Kahuna Lane were formerly lined with wooden homes for families and bungalows for bachelors and on any given day, one could see peddlers carrying their wares through the community in baskets slung over their shoulders on bamboo poles as they cried out, "Manapua! Crackers! Candy!"

PEACH CUSTARD CAKE

Serves 9-12

1 1/2 cups flour
1/2 teaspoon salt
1/2 cup margarine, softened
1 can (29 oz.) sliced peaches, well drained and save 1/4
        cup syrup
1/4 cup sugar
1/4 teaspoon cinnamon
1 egg, slightly beaten
1 cup evaporated milk

Combine flour and salt; cut in margarine with pastry blender or two knives. Press mixture firmly into bottom and half-way up sides of 8-inch square pan. Arrange drained peaches on crust in pan. Combine sugar and cinnamon in bowl and sprinkle over peaches. Bake at 375°F. for 20 minutes.

Mix reserved syrup, egg and milk; pour over peaches. Bake additional 30 minutes or until custard is firm, except in center which becomes firm upon standing. Serve warm or cold.

MOIST MANGO CAKE

Serves About 24

A delicious cake from the Ilikai Hotel's former Executive Chef (circa 1974)

2 cups sugar
1 1/2 teaspoons salt
2 teaspoons baking soda
4 teaspoons baking powder
2 cups cake flour, sifted
2 cups salad oil
5 eggs, beaten
1 1/2 cups chopped ripe mangoes
1 teaspoon vanilla extract
1 cup evaporated milk
1/2 cup water

Mix together sugar, salt, baking soda, baking powder, flour, oil and eggs on slow speed of mixer for 3 minutes. Add mangoes, vanilla, milk and water; mix at slow speed for additional minute. Pour batter into greased 9 x 13 x 2-inch pan or two 9-inch cake pans. Bake at 365°F. 30 minutes or until wooden pick inserted in center of cake comes out clean. (Chef Wuest used to bake this cake at this odd temperature because it keeps the cake extremely moist). Delicious eaten plain but frost or serve with whipped cream, if desired.

OLD FASHIONED BANANA CAKE   Serves 20-24

1 box (18.5 oz) banana cake mix
3/4 teaspoon baking powder
1 1/2 cup mashed ripe bananas (about 3 medium)
3 eggs
1/2 cup water
1/3 cup canola or salad oil
1/2 cup chopped nuts

Topping:
1/2 cup flour
1/2 cup sugar
1/4 cup butter or margarine, softened

To prepare cake, combine ingredients in large mixing bowl. Blend at low speed until completely moistened, about 1 minute. Beat 2 minutes at medium speed. Spread batter in a greased and floured 13 x 9 x 2-inch pan.

To make Topping, mix all ingredients in a medium-sized bowl using a fork or pastry blender; mixture will be crumbly. Sprinkle mixture evenly over cake batter and bake at 350°F. 40-45 minutes, or until center springs back when lightly touched.

OLD FASHIONED DATE CAKE

Serves 8-10

2 cups flour
1 cup sugar
1/2 teaspoon salt
1 teaspoon baking soda
2 eggs, beaten
1/2 cup butter, melted
3/4 cup sour milk
1 cup dates

Topping:
1 orange
1/2 cup sugar

Prepare cake by mixing together flour, sugar, salt and baking soda until well blended. In separate bowl, mix together eggs, butter and milk. Pour dry mixture into liquid mixture and beat slightly until mixed; add dates. Bake in nonstick 8 x 8-inch pan at 350°F. 40-45 minutes.

To prepare Topping, grate rind of orange and mix well with the juice of the orange and sugar. Let stand. When cake is done, poke holes in top with a fork and pour orange topping over hot cake. Keep cake in pan until ready to serve.

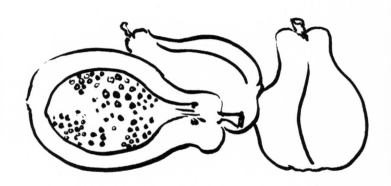

ONO COCONUT CAKE

Serves 8-10

3 cups cake flour
1 1/2 cups sugar
1 2/3 tablespoons baking powder
1/2 teaspoon salt
8 egg whites
1 1/2 cups fresh or canned coconut milk
1 1/2 cups fresh or packaged grated coconut

Sift together flour, sugar and baking powder. Add salt to egg whites and beat until stiff but not too dry. Add coconut milk to dry ingredients and beat until smooth. Fold in grated coconut and egg whites. Pour into two greased and floured 9-inch cake pans; bake at 350°F. 35-40 minutes or until inserted knife comes out clean.

Cool and frost with white frosting of your choice. Sprinkle generously with more grated coconut, if desired.

Benjamin J. Cayetano
Governor
State of Hawaii

PUMPKIN-PINEAPPLE CAKE

Serves 20-24

2 cups flour
2 teaspoons baking powder
1/2 teaspoon baking soda
1/2 teaspoon salt
1 teaspoon ground cinnamon
1/2 teaspoon nutmeg
1/8 teaspoon ground ginger
1 cup sugar
1/2 cup brown sugar, packed
1 cup canola oil
3 eggs
1 cup canned pumpkin
1 can (8 oz.) crushed pineapple in unsweetened juice
1 1/2 cups bite-sized crispy wheat squares cereal,
        crushed to 1/2 cup

Frosting:
1/4 cup butter or margarine, softened
2 1/2 cups powdered sugar, sifted
1 teaspoon vanilla extract
1-2 tablespoons milk

1/2 cup chopped nuts

Mix together flour, baking powder, baking soda, salt, cinnamon, nutmeg and ginger. In a separate bowl, combine white and brown sugar; add oil and mix well. Beat in eggs, then add pumpkin, undrained pineapple and cereal; mix thoroughly. Add flour mixture and mix until well combined. Pour into greased 12 x 9-inch baking pan. Bake at 350°F. 30-35 minutes or until top springs back when lightly touched.

To make Frosting, combine butter and sugar in medium bowl. Beat in vanilla and enough milk to make a smooth frosting. Spread on cooled cake and sprinkle with chopped nuts.

RED VELVET CAKE
Serves 8-10

This recipe became famous because, according to one ac-count, a woman enjoyed this cake so much that she asked for the recipe and was given it. However, she also received a bill for a few hundred dollars for the recipe. Needless to say, the woman was so angered by it that she decided to share the recipe with as many people as possible! Thus, you have it now, so enjoy!

1 cup butter or margarine
1 1/2 cups sugar
2 eggs
1/2 teaspoon salt
2 tablespoons cocoa
2 1/2 cups cake flour
1 1/4 teaspoons baking soda
1 cup buttermilk
1 bottle (1 oz.) red food color

Cream Cheese Frosting:
4 ounces cream cheese, softened
3 tablespoons unsalted butter, softened
1 1/2 cups confectioners' sugar, sifted
1/2 teaspoon vanilla extract
Juice of 1/4 lemon

Cream butter and sugar until light and fluffy. Add eggs, one at a time, beating well after each addition. Sift dry ingredients together; add to butter mixture alternately with buttermilk and food coloring beginning and ending with flour. Pour batter into two lightly greased and floured 8 or 9-inch layer pans. Bake at 350°F. 30-35 minutes. Frost with Cream Cheese Frosting or your favorite Butter Cream Frosting.

To prepare Cream Cheese Frosting, cream together cream cheese and butter; slowly add confectioners' sugar and continue beating until fully incorporated and smooth. Stir in vanilla and lemon juice.

RHUBARB STREUSEL CAKE
Serves 9-12

1 egg, beaten
1 cup sugar
1/4 cup margarine or butter, melted and cooled
1 cup buttermilk or sour milk
2 cups all purpose flour
1 teaspoon baking powder
1/2 teaspoon baking soda
1/4 teaspoon salt
2 cups chopped rhubarb

Topping:
1/3 cup sugar
2 tablespoons flour
2 tablespoons margarine or butter, melted

Vanilla Sauce:
1/2 cup sugar
1/2 cup margarine or butter
1/2 cup evaporated milk
2 tablespoons vanilla extract

Beat egg, sugar and margarine or butter together; stir in buttermilk. Combine flour, baking powder, baking soda and salt; add to buttermilk mixture, stirring just until combined. Fold in rhubarb. Spread into greased 9 x 9 x 2-inch baking pan.

Combine sugar, flour and margarine or butter for Topping and sprinkle over batter. Bake at 350°F. 45 minutes. Cool in pan or on wire rack.

To make Vanilla Sauce, combine sugar, margarine or butter and milk; bring to a boil then reduce heat. Cook gently over medium heat 8-10 minutes, stirring occasionally. Stir in vanilla; cool to room temperature. Stir and drizzle over cake.

SOUR CREAM COFFEE CAKE

Serves 8-10

1/2 cup butter or margarine
1 cup sugar
2 eggs
1 cup sour cream
1 teaspoon vanilla
2 cups flour
1 teaspoon baking soda
1 teaspoon baking powder
Pinch of salt

Topping:
1/2 cup chopped nuts
1 teaspoon ground cinnamon
1/4 cup sugar

Cream butter and sugar. Add sour cream, eggs and vanilla to butter mixture with dry ingredients which have been sifted together. Mix well and pour one-half of batter into greased 9 or 10-inch tube pan. Combine Topping ingredients and pour one-half over batter in pan. Pour remaining half of batter in pan and cover with remaining topping. Bake at 350°F. 45 minutes or until inserted toothpick comes out clean.

WATERGATE CAKE

Serves 20-24

1 package (18.5 oz.) white or yellow cake mix
1 package (3.5 oz.) instant pistachio pudding mix
3 eggs
3/4 cup canola or salad oil
1 cup lemon-lime soda

Icing:
2 envelopes (1 1/2 oz. each) nondairy whipped topping
**   mix**
1 package (3 1/2 oz.) instant pistachio pudding mix
1 1/2 cups milk

Combine cake mix, pudding mix, eggs, oil and soda in bowl and beat until well blended. Pour mixture into a greased and floured 9 x 13-inch baking pan and bake at 350°F. 35-45 minutes or until done. Cool and frost.

To prepare Icing, beat all ingredients in bowl until smooth and thick. Spread over cooled cake.

Have Your Cake and Eat It, Too

Dessert can be an every day event if you watch portion sizes and experiment with creative ways to cut fat without sacrificing flavor. When baking your own treats, try these low-fat substitutions:

• Use cake or pastry flour instead of all-purpose flour to maintain moistness that is sometimes lost when following a fat-free recipe. Cake flour also enhances tenderness and delivers a product with a fine grain and texture.

• Use unsweetened cocoa powder instead of baking chocolate. Two ounces of baking chocolate equal 1/3 cup unsweetened cocoa powder.

• Replace traditional ingredients with "mini" versions. For example, 1/2 cup mini chocolate chips works the same as 1 cup of full-sized chips.

• Use two egg whites instead of one whole egg.

• Use 1 cup buttermilk instead of whole milk.

• Use 1/2 cup marshmallow creme instead of 1/2 cup butter in frostings.

• Use 1/2 cup unsweetened applesauce or pureed prunes instead of 1/2 cup oil. Prunes taste best in spicy treats such as gingerbread; applesauce works best in heavier desserts.

• Replace 1 cup whipped cream with 1 cup non-dairy light whipped topping.

• Replace cream cheese with low-fat or fat-free versions or pureed nonfat cottage cheese.

COOKIES

BANANA BARS WITH
ORANGE BUTTER ICING

Makes 3-4 Dozen

4 eggs
2 cups mashed ripe bananas
1 2/3 cups sugar
1 cup vegetable oil
2 cups all purpose flour
2 teaspoons baking powder
1 teaspoon baking soda
1 teaspoon salt
2 teaspoons ground cinnamon

Orange Butter Icing:
1/4 cup butter, softened
3 cups powdered sugar
1/4 cup orange juice

In a large bowl, beat together eggs, bananas, sugar and oil. In a separate bowl, stir together flour, baking powder, baking soda, salt and cinnamon; add to the banana mixture; mix well. Spread evenly on an ungreased cookie sheet. Bake at 350°F. 25-30 minutes or until done. Allow to cool.

To prepare Orange Butter Icing, cream butter, add powdered sugar alternately with orange juice and mix until of smooth consistency. Spread on top of banana bars and let set until firm, about 15-30 minutes. Cut into squares or rectangles.

BEST CHOCOLATE
SYRUP BROWNIES
Makes 9-12

1/2 cup butter or margarine, softened
1 cup sugar
3 large eggs, beaten
1 cup all-purpose flour
Pinch of salt
3/4 cup chopped pecans or walnuts
3/4 cup chocolate syrup
2 teaspoons vanilla extract

Beat butter at medium speed of an electric mixer until fluffy. Add sugar, beating well. Add eggs one at a time, beating well after each addition. In a separate bowl, combine flour and salt. Add flour mixture to creamed mixture and beat well. Add chopped pecans, chocolate syrup, and vanilla. Pour into a greased and floured 9-inch square pan. Bake at 350°F. 35 minutes. Cool in pan on a wire rack. Cut into squares.

CHOCOLATE CHIP BARS
Makes 32 Bars

1/3 cup shortening
1/3 cup butter
1/2 cup sugar
1/2 cup brown sugar
1 egg
1 teaspoon vanilla extract
1 1/2 cups flour
1/2 teaspoon baking soda
1/2 teaspoon salt
1/2 cup chopped nuts
1 package (6 oz.) semi-sweet chocolate chips

Mix all ingredients and spread in an ungreased 9 x 13-inch pan. Bake at 375°F. 20-25 minutes. Cool and cut into 3 x 1-inch bars.

CHRISTMAS BARS

Makes 32 Bars

> **1/4 cup butter, softened**
> **1 cup sugar**
> **2 eggs**
> **1 1/4 cups biscuit mix**
> **1 cup fruit cake mix**
> **1/4 cup chopped nuts**
> **1/4 cup chopped dates**
> **1/4 cup chopped cherries**

Mix together butter and sugar, then add eggs and mix well. In separate bowl, gently mix remaining ingredients. Combine butter mixture with dry mixture and spread in greased 9 x 13-inch pan. Bake at 350°F. 30-35 minutes. Cool slightly before cutting into 1 1/2-inch squares.

CRUNCHY COOKIES

Makes 5 Dozen

> **2 1/4 cups all purpose flour**
> **1 teaspoon baking soda**
> **1 teaspoon baking powder**
> **1/2 cup hydrogenated shortening**
> **1/2 cup (1 block) butter or margarine**
> **1 tablespoon peanut butter, optional**
> **3/4-1 cup brown sugar, packed**
> **3/4-1 cup white sugar**
> **2 eggs, beaten**
> **1 teaspoon vanilla extract**
> **2 cups quick oats**
> **2 cups toasted rice cereal**
> **1/2 cup chopped nuts, optional**

Sift together flour, baking soda and baking powder; set aside. Cream together shortening, butter or margarine, peanut butter and sugars until well blended. Add eggs, one at a time, mixing well after each addition. Add vanilla and dry ingredients; mix just until smooth. Stir in cereals and nuts. Drop walnut-sized dough onto greased cookie sheets; press tops to flatten slightly. Bake at 350°F. 20 minutes or until lightly browned. Cool and store in air tight container.

LEILANI BARS

1/2 cup butter or margarine
1 1/2 cups sugar
4 eggs, beaten
1 1/2 cups flour
1/2 teaspoon baking soda
1 can (No. 2) crushed pineapple
1/2 cup chopped nuts
1/2 cup shredded coconut

Melt butter or margarine and mix with sugar and eggs. Add dry ingredients. Mix in pineapple, nuts, and coconut. Put mixture into greased 9 x 13-inch pan. Bake at 350°F. 30-45 minutes.

Variations:
Add chopped guava rind, pitted surinam cherries, or chopped mango.

OATMEAL CRISPIES

Makes 4 Dozen

1/2 cup butter
1 cup sugar
1 cup brown sugar, packed
2 eggs, beaten well
1 teaspoon vanilla extract
1 teaspoon baking soda
1 teaspoon salt
3 cups flour
3 cups instant oatmeal

Thoroughly cream butter and sugars. Add eggs and vanilla extract; mix well. Sift together baking soda, salt and flour; add to creamed mixture. Add oatmeal and mix together until stiff. If not quite stiff, add additional flour until you can form 3/4 inch balls in your hands without sticking. Place balls on cookie sheet, 1 dozen per sheet, using a large fork to press each ball down and flatten slightly. Bake at 350°F. 18 to 19 minutes. Remove from oven and allow to cool.

Note: Will keep well in well-sealed container.

PINEAPPLE BARS

Makes 24-32 Bars

1/2 cup margarine, melted
2 cups sugar
4 large eggs
1 1/2 cup flour
1/2 teaspoon salt
1/2 teaspoon baking soda
1 cup chopped walnuts
1 can (No. 2) crushed Hawaiian pineapple
Confectioner's sugar, optional

Drain pineapple well. Cool the melted butter and add sugar. Beat eggs until thick; cream with butter and sugar.

Sift together flour, salt and baking powder; add to creamed mixture. Add pineapple and nuts. Mix well and pour into greased 13 x 9 x 2-inch pan. Bake at 350°F. 30 minutes. Sprinkle with confectioner's sugar, if desired.

Mrs. Helene Matsunaga
Wife of the late U.S. Senator Sparky Matsunaga

PINEAPPLE NUT BARS   **Makes 24-32 Bars**

1/2 cup butter
2 cups sugar
4 eggs
1 1/2 cups flour
1/2 teaspoon baking soda
1 can (No. 2) crushed pineapple, drained well
Pinch of salt
1 tablespoon powdered sugar
1 cup chopped walnuts

Soften butter at room temperature. Cream butter and sugar, then add eggs, one at a time, mixing well after each addition. Combine flour, baking soda and salt. Add dry ingredients alternately with crushed pineapple to creamed butter mixture. Pour batter into greased and floured 14 x 10 x 2-inch pan; bake at 350°F. 35-40 minutes. Cool and sprinkle with powdered sugar.

Carol Shiraki
Carol's Bake Shop

PIES

BLUEBERRY CREAM CHEESE PIE
Serves 6-8

1 package (8 oz.) cream cheese, softened
3/4 cup confectioner's sugar
1 teaspoon vanilla
1 cup heavy cream
1 can (20 oz.) blueberry pie filling, chilled
10-inch baked pie shell

Thoroughly blend cream cheese, sugar and vanilla. Whip heavy cream until stiff; fold into cream cheese mixture and pour into cooled pie shell. Top with blueberry pie filling. Chill for several hours in refrigerator before serving.

LEMON TOFU PIE
Makes Two 8-inch Pies

1 box (6 oz.) lemon flavored gelatin
2 cups hot water
1/4 cup lemon juice
1 block (20 oz.) soft tofu
2-3 drops lemon extract
2 containers (8 oz. each) nondairy whipped topping
2 8-inch ready-made butter flavored graham pie crusts

Combine gelatin, hot water and lemon juice; beat with mixer; refrigerate until thickened and of syrup consistency, about 20-30 minutes. In a separate bowl, beat tofu until smooth. Mix in lemon extract and whipped topping; fold into thickened gelatin mixture and pour into pie crusts. Refrigerate until firm, about 3-4 hours. If desired, garnish with additional whipped topping.

Variations:
Any flavored gelatin may be substituted for lemon; delete lemon extract.

COCONUT CREAM PIE　　Serves 6-8

2 cups milk
1 cup sugar
1/4 teaspoon salt
1/4 cup grated coconut
4 egg yolks
3 tablespoons cornstarch
1 tablespoon butter
1 teaspoon vanilla extract
2 drops almond extract

1 baked 9-inch pie shell
Sweetened whipped cream, optional

Combine milk, 1/2 cup sugar, salt and coconut in double boiler and heat to near boiling. Mix together egg yolks, remaining 1/2 cup sugar and cornstarch; add to milk mixture and cook until thickened. Add butter, vanilla and almond extract. Cool and pour into baked pie shell. Top with whipped cream and additional coconut, if desired.

The Original Waioli Tea Room Restaurant (1974)

STRAWBERRY TOFU PIE　　Serves 6-8

1 package (3 oz.) strawberry flavored gelatin
1 cup boiling water
1/2 block soft tofu, drained well in colander
1 teaspoon lemon extract
1 teaspoon lemon juice
1 carton (8 oz.) non-dairy whipped topping, set aside 1 tablespoon for topping
1 8-inch ready-made graham pie crust

Dissolve gelatin in boiling water; chill 20 minutes. Blend gelatin, drained tofu, whipped topping, lemon juice and lemon extract until thoroughly mixed. Pour mixture into pie crust. Chill 3-4 hours or until set and top with remaining 1 tablespoon nondairy topping.

CUSTARD PIE

Makes 1 Pie

Pie Shell:
2 1/4 cups flour
1/4 teaspoon salt
3 teaspoons sugar
3/4 cup vegetable oil
3 tablespoons milk

Filling:
2 3/4 cups milk (1 one-quart package of powdered milk
and enough water to make 2 3/4 cups)
8 extra large eggs
2 additional egg yolks
3/4 to 1 cup sugar
1/4 teaspoon salt
1/2 teaspoon vanilla
1/8 teaspoon nutmeg

To make Pie Shell, place dry ingredients into 10-inch metal pie pan (glass or aluminum foil pan will not result in crisp, brown crust). Stir with fork. Whip milk and oil in measuring cup together with fork. Pour oil/milk mixture into dry ingredients, mix pat out, and flute. Bring sides of crust up as high as possible. If you have the time, refrigerate the crust. Alternatively, you can make ahead of time, freeze, and defrost before adding filling.

To make Filling, scald milk very thoroughly. Beat together eggs, egg yolks, sugar, salt, vanilla, and nutmeg. Pour scalded milk into mixture, stirring constantly. Pour half of custard mixture into Pie Shell. Place in 450°F. oven and bake until filling begins to set. Pour remainder of custard mixture into pie shell. If you can't get it all in, wait 10 minutes and try again with the last 1/2 cup or so. When the edges of the filling begin to set, they will be able to hold additional filling. Bake at 450° F. for 13 minutes. Lower heat to 400°F. and continue baking for 12 to 16 minutes. Be sure to watch closely for the last 8 minutes. At first the surface will slosh if you jiggle the pie. As soon as it sets up like gelatin, test with a metal knife. Pie is done when the knife comes out clean.

SHORTBREAD PUMPKIN PIE

Serves 16-24

Crust:
1 cup butter, softened
1/2 cup sugar
3 cups flour

Filling:
4 eggs, slightly beaten
1 large can (29 oz.) solid pack pumpkin
1 1/2 cups sugar
1 teaspoon salt
1 teaspoon ground cinnamon
1/2 teaspoon ground cloves
1 teaspoon ground ginger
2 large cans (12 oz. each) evaporated milk

To prepare Crust, mix together butter, sugar and flour; press into lightly greased 9 x 13-inch pan. Bake at 425°F. 15 minutes. While Crust is baking prepare Filling by mixing together all the ingredients listed; mix well and pour over half-baked crust. Lower temperature to 350°F. and bake 50 minutes or until knife inserted in center comes out clean. If desired, serve with sweetened whipped cream or non-dairy whipped topping.

SWEET POTATO PIE
Serves 8-10

---

2 eggs, separated
3/4 cup brown sugar, packed
1 1/2 cups boiled sweet potatoes, mashed
2 cups milk
2 tablespoons butter, melted
1 teaspoon cinnamon, nutmeg or pumpkin pie spice
1/2 teaspoon baking powder
Pinch of salt

1 tub (4 oz.) whipped topping

Beat egg whites until stiff; set aside. Beat egg yolks with sugar; add to potatoes with milk, melted butter and spice. Fold in egg whites, baking powder and salt and pour into pastry-lined pie pan. Bake at 350°F. 45 minutes or until knife inserted in center comes out clean. Top cooled pie with whipped topping to serve.

Note: Top pie with a layer of haupia for that extra special touch!

TWO TONE HOLIDAY PUMPKIN PIE
Serves 8-10

---

1 9-inch unbaked pie shell
1 cup canned mincemeat
1 can (18 oz.) solid pack pumpkin
1/4 cup orange juice
1 cup evaporated milk, undiluted
1/2 teaspoon grated orange peel
Whipping cream, whipped

Spread mincemeat over bottom of pie shell. Prepare pumpkin pie filling as directed on the label except substitute the orange juice and evaporated milk for the liquid specified in the directions. Stir in orange peel and pour over mincemeat in pie shell. Bake at 450°F. 10 minutes,

---

then at 350°F. for 50 minutes longer, or until a knife inserted in middle of pie comes out clean. Garnish with whipped cream.

WAIOLI APPLE PIE
Serves 6-8

4 cups fresh apple slices
1 1/2 cups sugar
1/8 teaspoon salt
1/4 teaspoon nutmeg
1/4 teaspoon cinnamon
1 tablespoon lemon juice
1/2 teaspoon instant coffee
3 tablespoons flour
2 tablespoons butter

Pastry for 9-inch Two Crust Pie

Combine all ingredients in a bowl; mix well and pour into pastry lined pie pan; dot with butter. Cover with top crust that has slits cut in it; seal and flute. Cover edge with 2-to 3-inch strip of foil to prevent excessive browning. Remove foil during last 15 minutes of baking. Bake at 375°F. 45-60 minutes or until crust is brown and juice begins to bubble through slits in crust. Serve hot with slice of cheese or pour cinnamon sauce over.

The Original Waioli Tea Room Restaurant (1974)

THE WILLOWS COCONUT CREAM PIE   Serves 8-10

Filling:
2 cups milk
1/2 cup sugar
Pinch of salt
1/4 cup grated coconut
2 heaping tablespoons cornstarch
4 egg yolks
1 tablespoon butter
1 teaspoon vanilla extract

Meringue:
4-6 egg whites
Approximately 1 tablespoon sugar for each egg white
Grated coconut

1 9-inch baked pie shell

Put milk, sugar, salt and grated coconut in saucepan; let come to near-boil; mix cornstarch and egg yolks together with a little water and add to milk mixture, stirring continually, until thickened on low heat; add butter and vanilla. Cool and fill pie shell. Beat egg whites until frothy; add sugar gradually and beat until stiff but not dry. Spread over cooled cream filling, sealing to edges of pastry. Sprinkle coconut over top. Bake at 400°F. until brown, about 2-3 minutes.

Willows Restaurant (1954)

After World War II, the Hausten family opened The Willows Restaurant on the family homestead. Colorful carp frolicked in the natural springs which flowed through old underground lava tubes, since sealed, between the quarry and the homestead. The Willows, with its thatched roof and lush tropical flora, offered a charm and hospitality reminiscent of an earlier era to Islanders and visitors for many years.

DESSERTS

BANANA CREAM SQUARES
Serves 24

Crust:
2 cups flour
2 tablespoons sugar
1 cup butter, softened

Filling:
1 package (8 oz.) cream cheese
2 boxes (3.5 oz.) instant vanilla pudding
3 cups milk
1 large container (16 oz.) non-dairy whipped topping
6 medium-sized ripe bananas, sliced

To make crust, combine flour, sugar, and butter and press into 9 x 13-inch cake pan. Bake at 325°F. for 15 minutes.

To make Filling, beat cream cheese until softened. Whip pudding and milk until thickened. Add to the creamed cheese; mix well and spread over baked crust. Lay the sliced bananas on top and cover with whipped topping. Refrigerate 3-4 hours before serving.

BUTTER MOCHI
Makes 24-32 Pieces

1/2 cup butter
2 2/3 cups sugar
4 eggs, beaten
4 cups mochiko
2 teaspoons baking powder
1 can (12 oz.) coconut milk
2 cups milk
1 teaspoon vanilla extract

Cream butter and sugar. Add eggs. Alternately add remaining liquids and dry ingredients and mix thoroughly. Pour into 9 x 13 x 2-inch baking pan and bake at 350° F. for 1 hour 15 minutes.

BAVARIAN TART

Serves 20-24

Crust:
1 cup butter
2/3 cup sugar
1/2 teaspoon vanilla
1 1/2 cups flour
1 cup chopped nuts

Filling:
2 packages (8 oz. size) cream cheese
2 eggs
1/2 cup sugar
1 teaspoon vanilla

2 cans (29 oz. size) bartlett pears
Cinnamon

To prepare crust, cream butter and sugar; add vanilla then the flour and nuts. Mix well and press into bottom of 9 x 13-inch pan. Bake at 350°F. 12-15 minutes or until edges are brown. Set aside and let cool.

To prepare Filling, beat cheese until softened; beat in eggs. Add sugar and vanilla; cream until smooth; do not overbeat or mixture will get watery. Pour cheese mixture into cooled crust; set aside. Slice pears into wedges and arrange over cheese filling; sprinkle cinnamon over pears and bake at 350°F. 40 minutes.

BIBINGKA (Coconut Rice Cake)

Makes 24-32 Pieces

4 cups mochiko
1 tablespoon baking powder
4 cups coconut milk
1 1/2 cups brown sugar, packed
1 teaspoon vanilla

Mix mochiko and baking powder in a bowl. Gradually add

the coconut milk. Add sugar and vanilla; mix well. Line 9 x 13-inch pan with 2 or 3 layers of banana leaves. Trim leaves at the rim of the pan. Brush coconut milk on leaves to prevent dough from sticking; pour mochiko mixture into pan and bake at 300°F. for 20 minutes or until slightly dry. Brush surface with coconut milk. Return to oven and bake for another hour.

BROKEN GLASS GELATIN

Serves 20-24

5 boxes (3 oz. each) flavored gelatin, different flavors
5 cups hot water
7 packets plain gelatin
3 cups warm skim milk
1 cup sugar

Sweetened whipped cream, optional

Separately dissolve each box of flavored gelatin with 1 cup hot water; add 1/2 packet of plain gelatin to each mixture. Mix each until completely dissolved; refrigerate until firm.

In separate bowl, mix warm skim milk with sugar and 4 packets plain gelatin; mix until completely dissolved; let cool to room temperature. Slice each chilled flavored gelatin into cubes or desired shapes and sizes; arrange in greased 9 x 13-inch pan. Pour cooled milk mixture over flavored gelatin pieces; refrigerate until firm. Serve with sweetened whipped cream, if desired.

COFFEE MOLD

Serves About 10-12

1 cup milk
2 1/2 packages unflavored gelatin
3/4 cup boiling water
4 teaspoons instant coffee crystals
3/4 cup sugar
1/4 teaspoon salt
2 eggs
1 bottle (8 oz.) whipping cream

Combine milk and gelatin in blender and let stand 1 minute. Add 1/2 cup boiling water and blend 20-30 seconds. Add remaining 1/4 cup hot water and instant coffee; blend additional 20-30 seconds. Add sugar, salt, eggs and whipping cream; blend until well mixed, about 10-20 seconds. Pour into desired mold and refrigerate until firm, about 4-6 hours.

CUSTARD MOCHI

Makes 24-32 Pieces

1/2 cup butter
1 3/4 cups sugar
4 large eggs
4 cups milk
2 teaspoons vanilla
2 cups mochiko
1 tablespoon baking powder

Cream butter and sugar. Beat in eggs one at a time. Add remaining ingredients and pour into a greased 9 x 13-inch pan. Bake at 350°F. 1 hour.

DATE BALLS
Makes about 24

3/4 cup sugar
2 eggs
1 1/2 cups chopped dates
Vanilla extract
Almond extract
2 cups toasted rice cereal
Shredded coconut

Mix sugar and eggs in frying pan over low heat. Add chopped dates and cook another 12 minutes. Add vanilla and almond extract. Add toasted rice cereal and form into balls. Roll in shredded coconut.

EASY MALASADAS
Makes 3 Dozen

1 cup milk
1 egg, beaten
1/2 teaspoon lemon extract
2 cups buttermilk baking mix
4 slices day old bread

1 quart canola oil for deep frying
1/2 cup sugar

Combine milk, egg and lemon extract. Add buttermilk mix and beat until smooth. Cut each slice of bread into 9 squares and dip into batter. Carefully drop each batter-coated square of bread into hot oil. Deep fry about 2 minutes or until golden brown. Drain on absorbent paper and roll in sugar.

EASY PEACH COBBLER
Serves 6-9

1/2 cup margarine
1 cup sugar
1 cup flour
1/2 - 2 teaspoons baking powder
1/4 teaspoon salt, optional
3/4 cup milk
1 can (29 oz.) peaches in syrup

Melt margarine in a microwave-safe baking dish. In mixing bowl, mix sugar, flour and baking powder; add milk. Pour mixture on top of melted butter but do not mix. Add peaches, syrup and all. Bake at 375°F. 40 minutes.

FRESH FRUIT DESSERT
Serves 18-24

Though the preparation of the recipe may be time consuming, it's well worth the effort for it is a very pretty and festive dessert.

Filo leaves
Melted butter
Panko flakes

Cream Cheese Mixture:
1 package (8 oz.) cream cheese
3/4 cup sugar
1 bottle (8 oz.) whipping cream, whipped
1 teaspoon vanilla extract

Fresh fruits (strawberries, kiwi, grapes, nectarine slices,
cherries mandarin oranges, etc.)

Thaw filo leaves in refrigerator for a minimum of 8 hours; remove from refrigerator and let stand 2 hours. Layer 6 filo leaves on a cookie sheet, brushing with melted butter and sprinkling panko flakes on each leaf. Poke random holes in leaves and bake at 350°F. about 15-20 minutes or until light brown. Cut into squares or diamond shapes and allow to cool.

To make Cream Cheese Mixture, cream sugar and cream cheese; fold in whipped cream and vanilla extract. Spread on filo pieces and garnish with fresh fruits.

Gwynne Nakamura
Carol's Bake Shop

GURI GURI SHERBET

Serves 10

2 cans (12 oz. size) strawberry soda
1 can (14 oz.) sweetened condensed milk
1 small can evaporated milk
1 can (12 oz.) lemon-lime soda

Combine and mix all ingredients, except lemon-lime soda, together. Freeze in 9 x 13-inch pan until semi-frozen. Scrape out and place in bowl; beat in 1 can lemon-lime soda. Pour into individual serving cups and refreeze until firm, about 2-3 hours.

HAUPIA

Makes 24-32 Pieces

1 quart milk
1 can (12 oz.) coconut milk
1 1/2 cups sugar
2 cups cornstarch
3 cups water

Mix milk, coconut milk and sugar together in stainless steel pot. In a separate bowl, mix together cornstarch and water to make paste. Bring milk mixture to a boil and briskly stir in cornstarch mixture until mixture comes to a boil again. Pour into 9 x 12-inch pan and cool, then refrigerate to set. When set, cut into pieces.

Randy Chee
Aloha Poi Bowl

ICE CAKE   **Makes About 1 Dozen Cups**

Before the days of flavored ices which are available today, ice cake was one of the favorite snacks for youngsters—especially on hot summer days. They were not only made at home but also sold at the neighborhood stores.

> **4 1/2 cups water**
> **1 1/2 cups sugar**
> **1 can (12 oz.) evaporated milk**
> **1 1/2 teaspoons flavor extract**
> **1 teaspoon food coloring**

Combine sugar and water in saucepan and bring to a boil; reduce heat and simmer until sugar dissolves. Add remaining ingredients; stir to combine thoroughly and pour into 4 oz. cups or ice trays and freeze.

Variations:
• Banana or lemon extract and yellow food coloring
• Mint extract with green food coloring
• Vanilla extract and no food coloring
• Vanilla extract and red food coloring

COFFEE ICE CAKE   **Makes About 1 Dozen Cups**

> **5 cups coffee**
> **1 1/2 cups sugar**
> **3/4 cup evaporated milk**

Combine coffee and sugar in a saucepan; bring to a boil. Reduce heat and cook until sugar dissolves; add milk and stir to mix thoroughly. Pour into 4-oz. cups or ice trays and freeze.

STRAWBERRY ICE CAKE

Makes About 1 Dozen Cups

4 1/2 cups water
1 1/2 cups sugar
3/4 cup evaporated milk
1/2 cup strawberry syrup

Combine water and sugar in a saucepan; bring to a boil. Reduce heat and cook until sugar dissolves; add milk and syrup, stir to mix thoroughly. Pour into 4-oz. cups or ice trays and freeze.

LAYERED MANJU

Makes 24-32 Pieces

5 cups flour
1/2 cup sugar
1/2 teaspoon salt
3/4 cup sweetened condensed milk
1 can (18 oz.) koshi-an
1 can tsubushi-an
1 pound butter, softened
1 egg, beaten

Mix dry ingredients together. In separate bowl, mix butter to soften. Mix dry ingredients into butter, alternately with milk. Divide dough in half; spread one half in 9 x 13-inch pan. Mix together the koshi-an and tsubushi-an and spread on dough. Spread other half of dough on -an mixture. Brush beaten egg over dough, but don't use all of the egg. Bake at 350°F. 40-45 minutes. Cool and cut into desired size.

Stone masons fashioned blocks from the Old Stone Quarry to construct many downtown Honolulu buildings, including historic Kawaiahao Church.

MICROWAVE CHICHI DANGO

Makes 24-30 Pieces

1 1/2 cups mochiko
1 1/2 cups water
1 cup sugar
Few drops red food coloring

Mix all ingredients together thoroughly. Place mixture into a greased 8 x 8-inch glass baking dish. Microwave on high for 7-8 minutes.

Note: If you do not have an automatic rotating microwave oven, you will need to turn the pan around after 4 minutes and complete the cooking.

OLD FASHIONED BREAD PUDDING

Serves 6-9

2 cups milk
1/4 cup butter or margarine
5 cups day old bread cubes
1/2 cup seedless raisins
3/4 cup sugar
2 eggs, beaten
1 teaspoon vanilla extract
1/2 teaspoon ground cinnamon

Place milk and butter in small saucepan and heat over low heat until scalded. Arrange bread cubes and raisins in non-stick 8-inch baking dish. Beat together milk mixture, sugar, eggs, vanilla and cinnamon. Pour over bread. Bake at 300°F. 45-50 minutes or until knife inserted into center of pudding comes out clean.

PEACH BAVARIAN

1 package (3 oz.) lemon flavored gelatin
1/2 package plain gelatin
2 tablespoons sugar
Pinch of salt
1 cup hot water
1 can (13 oz.) sliced peaches
1 cup heavy cream, whipped

Dissolve lemon and plain gelatin, sugar and salt in hot water. Drain peaches and add 1/2 cup of peach syrup to gelatin mixture. Pour 1/4 cup gelatin mixture in bottom of 1-quart mold. Arrange 10 peach slices in gelatin; chill. Chill remaining gelatin mixture in separate bowl until slightly thickened; fold in whipped cream. Cut remaining peaches in half and fold into cream mixture. Pour into mold over solidified gelatin and chill until firm, about 2-3 hours. Unmold on serving plate; garnish with mint leaves.

PEANUT BUTTER CRUNCHIES

1 box (18.25 oz.) devil's food cake mix
1 package (10 oz.) miniature marshmallows
2 cups creamy peanut butter
1 package (12 oz.) semi-sweet chocolate chips
2 cups puffed rice cereal

Mix cake according to box instructions. Pour into 2 greased 9 x 13-inch pans. Bake at 350°F. 15 minutes. Arrange marshmallows over cake and bake for additional 3 minutes. Melt peanut butter and chocolate chips together; mix in rice cereal. Pour over cooled cake and refrigerate until set.

PIE CRUST MANJU

> **6 cups flour**
> **1/4-1/2 cup sugar, optional**
> **1 1/2 teaspoons salt**
> **2 cups vegetable oil**
> **1 cup ice water**
> **1 can (18 oz.) tsubushi-an**
> **Evaporated milk**

Sift together flour, sugar and salt. Add oil and water; mix well. Form dough into walnut-size balls; flatten and fill with tsubushi-an and pinch edges together to seal. Place on lightly greased cookie sheet, seam side down. Brush tops of manju with evaporated milk. Bake at 425°F. for 20-25 minutes or until golden brown.

Variations:
Apple Manju - substititue canned apple pie filling for tsubushi-an.

Sweet Potato Manju - substitute cooked Okinawan sweet potato or cooked yam for tsubushi-an.

POI MOCHI

> **1 pound poi**
> **2 cups water, approximately**
> **2 packages (10 oz. each) mochiko**
> **1 1/2 cups sugar**
> **1 quart canola oil for deep frying**

Combine and mix together all ingredients except oil, adding water slowly to mixture until of desired consistency (ie. thick muffin batter)   Drop by teaspoonfuls into oil heated to 365°-375°F and deep fry until outside is slightly crisp. Drain on absorbent paper before serving.

PUMPKIN CRUNCH

Serves 24-32

Layer 1:
1 can (29 oz.) solid packed pumpkin
1 can (12 oz.) evaporated milk
3 eggs, slightly beaten
1 cup sugar
1 teaspoon ground cinnamon

Layer 2:
1 box (18.25 oz.) yellow cake mix
1 cup chopped nuts
1 cup melted butter

Topping:
1 package (8 oz.) cream cheese
1/2 cup powdered sugar
1/4 cup whipped cream

Mix together all ingredients for Layer 1. Pour mixture into wax paper lined 9 x 13-inch pan. Sprinkle top with 1 box yellow cake mix. Sprinkle and press chopped nuts on cake mixture then pour melted butter over nuts. Bake at 350°F. for 40-50 minutes or until knife inserted in center comes out clean. When done, cool. Turn over onto cake sheet and cool completely. Remove waxed paper. Beat Topping ingredients together and spread over cake.

The eight acres of the Honolulu Stadium land was converted to a public park through the community's hard work and united efforts ... an example of what can be achieved by people working together toward a common goal.

PUMPKIN PIE SQUARES

Serves 24-32

Crust:
1/2 cup sugar
3 cups flour
1 cup butter

Filling:
5 eggs, slightly beaten
1 large can (29 oz.) solid pack pumpkin
2 cups sugar
1 teaspoon salt
1 teaspoon cinnamon
1/2 teaspoon ground cloves
1 teaspoon ground ginger
2 cans (12 oz. size) evaporated milk

Mix together 1/2 cup sugar and flour; cut butter in with fork until mixture resembles coarse cornmeal; press into a greased 9 x 13-inch pan. Bake at 425°F. for 15 minutes. Mix together Filling ingredients and pour over baked crust; bake at 350°F. for 55 minutes or until knife inserted in center comes out clean.

Note: If thin crust is preferred, use half of recipe for crust.

PUMPKIN SQUARES WITH CREAM CHEESE FROSTING

Serves 24

1 can (16 oz.) solid pack pumpkin
1 2/3 cup brown sugar, firmly packed
4 eggs
3/4 cup vegetable oil
1 1/2 cups old fashioned oats, uncooked
1 tablespoon cinnamon
2 teaspoons baking powder
1 teaspoon baking soda
1 teaspoon salt

Cream Cheese Frosting:
1 package (3 oz.) cream cheese, softened
1/4 cup butter or margarine, softened
1 teaspoon vanilla extract
2 cups confectioner's sugar, sifted
1/2 cup chopped nuts, optional

To make pumpkin squares, combine pumpkin, sugar, eggs, and oil; mix until well blended. In separate bowl, combine remaining dry ingredients. Add this mixture to the pumpkin mixture and mix thoroughly. Pour into a greased 10 x 15-inch jelly roll pan, spreading evenly. Bake at 350°F 25-30 minutes or until wooden pick comes out clean. Remove from heat and allow to cool completely.

To make Cream Cheese Frosting, beat together cream cheese, butter, and vanilla until well blended. Gradually add confectioner's sugar, beating until smooth. Spread on top of pumpkin squares and sprinkle with nuts, if desired.

STEAMED MANJU   Makes About 12-18

3 1/2 cups flour
1 1/2 cups sugar
5 teaspoons baking powder
3 eggs, beaten
1/2 cup canola oil
1/2 cup milk
1 can (18 oz.) koshi-an

Sift or mix together dry ingredients. Combine eggs with oil and milk; pour slowly in dry ingredients. Mix together until well blended. Take small amounts of dough, about 1 tablespoon, and make indentation, placing a ball of koshi-an in the center; pinch edges together to seal. Place each manju on 2 x 2-inch wax paper squares; place in steamer and steam 10-15 minutes.

Pickles and Preserves

Jams and Jellies

Sauces and Gravies

Candies

Etc.,
Etc.,
Etc.

PICKLES & PRESERVES

BENI SHOGA
(Pickled Red Ginger)

    2 pounds fresh ginger
    Salt
    3/4 cup vinegar
    1 1/2 cups sugar
    1/3 cup water
    1/2 teaspoon red food coloring

Slice ginger crosswise into thin slices. Sprinkle with salt and let stand 2 hours. Combine remaining ingredients and bring to a boil. Set aside to cool. Drain but do not rinse ginger; squeeze out excess liquid and place in a jar. Pour sauce over ginger and refrigerate in covered jar.

TAKUWAN (Pickled Turnips)

    3/4 cup rice vinegar
    1 1/2 cups sugar
    3 tablespoons salt
    1/4 teaspoon yellow food coloring
    3-4 medium turnips, pared and cut into 1/2 x 2-inch strips
    1 red chili pepper, optional

Combine vinegar, sugar and salt in saucepan; bring to a boil and cook on low heat until sugar and salt dissolve; cool slightly. Add yellow coloring. Put turnip strips in a jar and pour hot vinegar mixture over; add pepper. Cool then cover jar and refrigerate 1-2 days before serving.

MANGO CHUTNEY

Makes About 6-8 Cups

12 cups green mango slices
2 tablespoons rock salt
2 cups cider vinegar
1/2 cup water
4 cups sugar
2 cups brown sugar, packed
1 cup raisins, optional
1/4 cup chopped fresh ginger
1 small onion, chopped
3 cloves garlic, minced or crushed
2 1/2 tablespoons (7-8 small) minced hot chili peppers
1/2 teaspoon ground cinnamon
1/4 teaspoon ground cloves
1/4 teaspoon nutmeg, optional
1/4 teaspoon allspice, optional

Sprinkle salt over mango slices and let stand overnight. Rinse and drain.

Combine sugars with vinegar and water; bring to a boil. Add remaining ingredients, except mangoes, and cook 15 minutes over medium heat. Add mangoes; simmer over low heat 30-45 minutes or until of desired consistency, stirring frequently to prevent sticking. Pour into hot sterilized jars and seal with paraffin.

Etc., Etc., Etc.

PEACH CHUTNEY

>5 pounds firm ripe peaches
>1/2 pound raisins
>1/2 pound chopped dates
>2 cups apple cider vinegar
>1 large lime
>3 cups sugar
>1/2 cup candied crystal ginger
>1/2 cup chopped pecans

Pare and dice peaches; add raisins, dates, and vinegar. Cut lime in quarters and remove seeds. Slice very thin and add to fruit mixture. Cook over medium heat, stirring occasionally, until peaches are tender. Add sugar and cook until thickened; stir often to prevent sticking. When mixture is thickened, add ginger and pecans. Stir and remove from heat. Pour into hot sterilized jars and seal with melted paraffin while still hot.

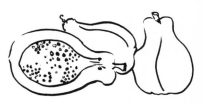

PICKLED GREEN PAPAYA

Serves 6

>1 medium green papaya, pared
>1/2 cup onion, thinly sliced
>2 teaspoons minced ginger
>1 clove garlic, minced
>2 Hawaiian red peppers, seeded and crushed
>1/4 cup cider vinegar
>3/4 teaspoon salt
>2 teaspoons sugar
>Dash of pepper

Cut papaya into halves and remove seeds; grate. Add onion, ginger, garlic and red pepper to papaya. Combine remaining ingredients and pour over papaya mixture; mix well. Cover and refrigerate overnight before serving.

PICKLED MANGOES   Makes 1 Gallon

   8 cups green mango slices
   2 cups sugar
   1 cup rice vinegar
   1/4 cup Hawaiian salt
   8 li hing mui

Place mango slices in a jar. Combine remaining ingredients in saucepan; bring to a boil; cool to lukewarm and pour over mangoes. Let stand 24 hours at room temperature then place in refrigerator.

PINEAPPLE CHUTNEY   Makes About 2 1/2 Quarts

   3 cans (1 lb. 4 oz. size) pineapple chunks
   4 cups brown sugar, packed
   3 cups cider vinegar
   2 cloves garlic, crushed or minced
   2 cups raisins
   2 cups currants, optional
   1 pound broken walnut pieces
   2 tablespoons crystallized ginger, chopped
   1/4 cup chopped onion
   1 tablespoon grated orange peel
   1 teaspoon salt
   1/2 teaspoon ground allspice
   1/2 teaspoon ground cinnamon
   2 teaspoons minced hot chili peppers
   1/4 teaspoon ground nutmeg

Combine all ingredients in a large saucepan and bring to a boil. Cook over medium heat 1 hour or until of desired consistency. Pour into hot sterilized jars and seal with paraffin.

Etc., Etc., Etc.

PRUNE MUI

Makes About 3 Quarts

> 5 pounds dried pitted prunes
> 1/2 pound dried lemon peel, chopped
> 1/2 pound li hing mui
> 1 pound dark brown sugar
> 1 1/2 cups lemon juice
> 1/4 cup whiskey
> 3 tablespoons rock salt
> 1 tablespoon Chinese five spice powder
> 8 whole cloves

Combine prunes, lemon peel and li hing mui in a large bowl. Combine remaining ingredients and pour over prunes, mixing thoroughly. Let stand 2 - 3 days before serving.

TSUKEMONO NO MOTO NO. 1

Makes 2 Cups Solution

Vegetables preserved in brine (tsukemono) are generally served as a side dish in the typical Japanese meal. Though every family has its own favorite recipe for sukemono, we'd like to share ours with you.

> 1 3/4 cups water
> 1 pieces (5 inches) dashi konbu
> 2 tablespoons rock salt
> 1 1/2 tablespoons sugar
> 1/2 teaspoon soy sauce
> 1 1/2 teaspoons rice vinegar
> 1 1/2 teaspoons sake
> 1/4 teaspoon MSG, optional

TSUKEMONO NO MOTO NO. 2   **Makes 9 Cups Solution**

1 cup brown sugar, packed
1/3 cup salt
1/4 cup rice vinegar
6 cups water
1/4 cup soy sauce
1 1/2 cups beer

TSUKEMONO NO MOTO NO. 3   **Makes 6 Cups Solution**

1 small box oatmeal
2 cans beer
2 cups brown sugar, packed
3/4 cup salt
2 teaspoons MSG, optional
1 piece (5 inches) dashi konbu

SUGGESTED VEGETABLES TO PICKLE: Turnips, radishes, head cabbage, cucumbers, eggplants, celery cabbage, Chinese mustard cabbage.

Combine all ingredients for Tsukemono No Moto of your choice and add desired vegetables. Let stand 1-2 days in refrigerator or at room temperature with 3-5 pound weight. Serve with soy sauce.

JAMS & JELLIES

EASY GUAVA JELLY   Makes About 10 (6 oz.) Jars

    3 1/2 cups guava juice
    1/2 cup lemon juice
    6 1/2 cups sugar
    1 pouch (3 oz.) liquid pectin

Combine juices and sugar in large saucepan; bring to a boil, stirring constantly. Immediately stir in pectin; bring to a boil and continue boiling over high heat 1 minute, stirring constantly. Remove from heat; skim foam and pour into hot sterilized jars; seal with melted paraffin while hot.

GUAVA JELLY   Makes About 2 Pints

    1 1/2 cans (12 oz. size) guava nectar base
    2 tablespoons water
    2 tablespoons lemon juice
    1 1/2 cups sugar

Thaw nectar base and pour into medium saucepan. Rinse the two cans with 2 tablespoons each of water and pour into saucepan. Cook over high heat until juice becomes thick; add lemon juice and sugar. Boil on high for another 13 minutes. To test if jelly is thickened enough, pour little in a plate. If the jelly hardens when cooled, it is ready. If not, cook another 5 minutes. Pour mixture in small sterilized jars and pour melted paraffin over to seal.

LILIKOI JELLY

Makes 3-4 (6 oz.)- Jars

1 cup water
3 1/4 cups sugar
1 pouch (3 oz.) liquid pectin
1/3 tablespoons lemon juice
1 can (6 oz.) frozen passion fruit juice, thawed

Combine water and sugar in a saucepan. Bring mixture to a boil and continue boiling over high heat 1 minute, stirring constantly. Turn heat off and immediately stir in pectin and juices. Skim foam and pour into hot sterilized jars; seal with melted paraffin while hot.

MANGO JAM

Makes 1 Pint

8 cups ripe mango slices
2 cups water
2 cups sugar
2 tablespoons lemon juice

Cook mango slices in water over low heat until tender. Press through strainer. Add sugar and lemon juice; cook slowly over low heat until of desired consistency for jam. Pour into hot sterilized jars and seal with paraffin or place in refrigerator for immediate use.

Moiliili was rezoned from agriculture to urban in the 1950's, allowing the construction of high-density apartments and condominiums.

PAPAYA-PINEAPPLE JAM

Makes About 3 Pints

3 cups chopped papaya
2 cups crushed pineapple
1/3 cup lemon juice
1/4 cup orange juice
1 teaspoon fresh ginger juice
Grated rind of 1 lemon
Sugar

Combine fruits, juices and rind in saucepan; cook 30 minutes, stirring occasionally. Measure cooked mixture; add equal amount of sugar and cook about 30 minutes or until mixture thickens, stirring frequently to prevent burning. Pour jam into hot sterilized jars and seal with melted paraffin while hot.

SAUCES & GRAVIES

BROWN GRAVY

2 tablespoons meat drippings (fat and juices)
2 tablespoons all-purpose flour
1 cup liquid (meat juices, broth, water)
1/4 teaspoon salt
1/4 teaspoon pepper
Browning sauce, optional

Pour drippings from pan into bowl, leaving brown particles in pan. Return 2 tablespoons drippings to pan. Stir in flour and cook over medium heat, stirring constantly, until flour is browned and mixture is smooth and bubbly; remove from heat. Stir in liquid and heat to boiling, stirring constantly. Boil and stir 1 minute. Stir in few drops of browning sauce, if desired. Add salt and pepper.

Variations:
Mushroom Gravy: Stir in 1 cup fresh, sliced mushrooms before adding flour or use 1 can (4 oz.) mushroom stems and pieces. Drain and use mushroom liquid for part of the liquid in gravy. Stir in 1/2 teaspoon Worcestershire sauce.

Onion Gravy: Stir in 1 cup onion slices before adding flour to drippings and cook onion slices until translucent.

Etc., Etc., Etc.

KOREAN STYLE BARBECUE SAUCE   Makes 1 1/4 Cups

1/2 cup soy sauce
1/2 cup sugar
1/4 cup sake
1 teaspoon salt
1 tablespoon sesame oil
1 teaspoon sesame seeds
1 slice ginger, mashed
1 clove garlic, mashed

Combine all ingredients and use as marinade for meats, poultry, and seafood.

SPICY BARBECUE SAUCE   Makes 2 Cups

This sauce is easy to prepare and delicious with shredded roasted beef brisket or pork tenderloin...especially good for spicy barbecue sandwiches!

2 tablespoons canola oil
1/2 cup chopped onion
1 tablespoon minced garlic
1 teaspoon ground cumin
1/4 teaspoon cayenne pepper
1 cup catsup
1/2 cup vinegar (malt vinegar preferred)
1/4 cup soy sauce
1/4 cup dark brown sugar, packed
2 tablespoons Worcestershire sauce
1/4 teaspoon liquid smoke flavoring

Heat oil in medium saucepan and sauté onion, garlic, cumin and pepper 3-4 minutes over medium heat. Stir in remaining ingredients and simmer, stirring constantly, until slightly thickened, about 8-10 minutes.

SU FOR SUSHI
(Seasoned Rice Vinegar)

Makes 1 Quart

2 cups sugar
2 cups rice vinegar
2 tablespoons salt
2 teaspoons MSG

Boil together and cool. Sprinkle over cooked hot rice and use for sushi of your choice.

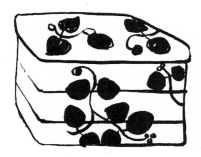

SUKIYAKI SAUCE

Makes 4 1/2 Cups

2 1/2 cups soy sauce
1 1/2 cups sugar
1/2 cup mirin

Combine ingredients and mix well. Store in glass jar for use as seasoning for Sukiyaki or other Japanese one-pot dishes.

TERIYAKI SAUCE   Makes 3 1/2 Cups

No. 1
2 cups soy sauce
1 cup brown sugar, packed
1 clove garlic, crushed
1 1/2 teaspoons grated fresh ginger
1/2 cup mirin

No. 2
2 cups soy sauce
2 cups sugar
1 clove garlic, crushed
1 1/2 teaspoons grated fresh ginger
1/2 cup mirin or sake

Combine ingredients in a jar; cover and shake until well blended. Use as marinade for beef, pork, poultry, lamb, fish and shellfish.

TOSA-ZU
(Seasoned Vinegar Sauce)   Makes 2 1/2 Quarts

This sauce keeps for 6-7 months in the refrigerator and improves with age. If the sauce seems strong for your taste, dilute portions of it with a little dashi. Keep the sauce handy for "instant" sunomono (vinegar flavored dishes). When used as a dressing for salads, add more dashi to the basic Tosa-Zu.

5 cups rice vinegar
3 cups dashi
1 cup mirin
1 cup soy sauce
1 1/2 cups sugar

Combine all ingredients in a saucepan; bring to a boil. Cool and keep refrigerated in covered jar.

Hiroshi Fukui, Executive Chef
L'Uraku Restaurant

YAKIDOFU WITH SAUCE

1 block tofu
3 eggs, beaten
Flour

Sauce:
1/3 cup shoyu
1 stalk green onion, chopped fine
1 thin sliced ginger, minced
1 clove garlic, minced
1 tablespoon sugar
1 tablespoon vinegar

Cut tofu lengthwise in half, then cut each half into slices about 1/3-inch thick. Lay slices on triple thickness of paper towels. Put in refrigerator to drain for a couple of hours. Turn over once. Combine ingredients to make sauce. Set aside. When ready to prepare tofu, flour each slice, dip in beaten egg and fry for about a minute on each side. Just before serving, spoon sauce over tofu.

CANDIES

EASY PECAN PRALINES
Makes About 12-18

> **3 cups sugar**
> **1/2 cup milk**
> **1 tablespoon butter**
> **1 1/2 cups pecans, halved**
> **1/2 teaspoon vanilla extract**

In medium sized heavy skillet (iron is best), using a wooden spoon, caramelize 1 cup sugar over low heat. In a heavy 2-quart saucepan, place remaining 2 cups sugar and milk; bring to a boil. Stir in caramelized sugar, butter and pecans; simmer 2 minutes. Remove from heat and add vanilla. Beat 2 minutes and drop onto wax paper, making certain a piece of pecan is in each piece of candy, that has been placed over newspaper. Allow to cool until hardened.

HAPA HAOLE
PUFFED RICE CANDY
Makes About 3 Dozen

> **1/2 cup toasted sesame seeds**
> **1/2 cup butter**
> **1 1/2 cups sugar**
> **1 teaspoon minced fresh ginger root**
> **1 cup salted peanuts**
> **7 cups puffed rice cereal**

Sprinkle one-half of the sesame seeds in a 15 1/2 x 10 1/2 x 1-inch baking pan. Melt butter in a wok or large kettle; add sugar. Cook over medium heat, stirring constantly, until sugar dissolves, about 10-15 minutes. Remove from heat and add ginger, peanuts and cereal, mixing well to coat cereal thoroughly. Quickly pour into prepared pan; spread and press to fit pan. Sprinkle remaining sesame seeds over surface and immediately cut into 2 x 1 1/2-inch pieces.

Notes

PART III
APPENDICES

Did You Know that in Ancient Times...

Mo'ili'ili was the site of a heiau built by Menehune, a race of small people that inhabited the Hawaiian Islands. According to Thomas Thrum's survey of ancient temple sites in 1907, Mauoki Heiau was a good sized temple, walled on three sides and open to the West. The stones for the construction were brought to this area by Menehune from Kawiwi in Wai'anae. The temple was located at the foot of the slope that divides Manoa from Palolo Valley. In 1883 Mauoki Heiau was torn down and the stones used for road work.

Glen Grant

THINGS WORTH SHARING ...

1. Most cookies are rich enough so that a greased cookie sheet is not necessary. If a cookie, which does not require a greased cookie sheet, is baked on a greased one, the cookie is likely to spread while baking and will have a deep brown, rather unattractive edge.

2. The ideal temperature for the rising of yeast dough is 80° to 85°F., which is about 10° warmer than ordinary room temperature.

3. To soften brown sugar, put it into a jar with a tight fitting cover. Place a very damp cloth in a dish on the sugar in the jar. Moisten the cloth often until sugar is soft or just pop it into your microwave oven for a few seconds.

4. Cut up dates and other sticky fruits with wet scissors. Dip scissors in water occasionally.

5. Condensed and evaporated milk should not be used interchangeably. Condensed milk is sweet and thick. Evaporated milk is ordinary milk from which about half the water has been removed; it has a consistency similar to cream.

6. Grated and ground nuts should not be used interchangeably. Grated nuts are fluffy and dry. They are sometimes used in place of flour in cookies and cakes. Ground nuts are more oily and compact.

7. When you have left-over egg yolks or egg whites, remember:
      1 egg yolk = about 1 tablespoon
      1 egg white = about 2 tablespoons

8. One pound of butter = 2 cups. One stick (1/4 pound) = 1/2 cup

9. To tint coconut, mix 1 tablespoon water and desired amount of food coloring in a quart jar. Add about 1 cup shredded coconut. Cover jar and shake until color is evenly distributed. Spread coconut on paper towel to dry.

10. If a gelatin mixture becomes too firm to fold in other ingredients, set bowl of gelatin in a pan of warm water until mixture is of desired consistency.

11. To make gravy, use 2 tablespoons each of drippings and flour for each cup of liquid.

12. Use only cooked or canned pineapple in gelatin mixtures. Raw or frozen pineapple prevents gelatin from congealing.

13. To help prevent a greenish ring around the yolk when eggs are cooked in the shell, cool them immediately in cold running water.

14. To help prevent a curdled appearance in escalloped potatoes, make a white sauce of 2 tablespoons each butter and flour for 1 cup milk. This is enough for 1 pound of potatoes.

15. As a time-saver, bake meatloaf in muffin pans at 450°F. for about 18 minutes.

16. One 6-ounce package semi-sweet chocolate chips equals about 1 cup.

17. Salting nuts: To 1 cup nuts in pan, add 1 teaspoon canola oil; stir. Brown at 325°F. or 350°F., stirring frequently. Drain and salt.

18. To toast nuts or coconut, heat in shallow pan at 325°F. or 350°F. until golden brown, stirring often.

19. Liquid shortening may not be substituted for solid shortening unless the recipe calls for melted shortening.

20. For accurate measurements, use a set of graduated measuring cups for measuring all dry ingredients. Use a glass measuring cup for liquid ingredients only.

21. Tint granulated sugar by adding one drop food coloring to about 1/3 cup sugar; mix and shake thoroughly. For minty flavor, add about 10 drops spearmint extract.

22. To blanch almonds, add boiling water to cover and let stand until skins are easily removed.

23. Almonds slice or cut most readily when warm and moist, immediately after being blanched.

24. Use a plastic or acrylic knife to cut mochi to prevent sticking.

25. Eggs separate best when cold and egg whites kept at room temperature beat up to its maximum volume when making meringue.

26. To prevent sliced bananas from turning brown, dip them in little a white wine or lemon juice - the acid in the wine or lemon prevents the fruit from oxidizing, but doesn't affect the flavor.

27. To prevent pie crust from browning too much, cut out the center of a disposable aluminum pie pan; cut out the bottom of the pan and save the resulting ring. Lay the aluminum ring on top of your crust during cooking if the edges are browning too quickly.

28. If ingredients bubble over onto the oven floor when baking, stop them from smoking by sprinkling the spillovers with salt. When baking is finished, scrape up the spill with a spatula immediately.

29. Seeds and nuts keep best and longest when stored in the freezer.

30. Add a little vinegar or lemon juice to potatoes before draining to make them extra white when mashed.

31. To avoid tears when cutting onions, try cutting them under cold running water or placing them in the freezer briefly before cutting.

32. To reduce odors when cooking cabbage, cauliflower and other cruciferous vegetables, add a little vinegar to the cooking water.

33. Dress up cooked vegetables by sprinkling them with toasted sesame seeds, chopped nuts, crumbled cooked bacon, canned French fried onions or slightly crushed seasoned croutons.

34. Use lemon juice to remove onion scent from hands.

GLOSSARY

aburage-deep fried tofu
adobo-Filipino vinegar flavored meat
ahi-Hawaiian name for yellowfin tuna
ajitsuke nori-seasoned seaweed
aku-Hawaiian name for skipjack tuna
an-red bean paste
andagi-Okinawan doughnut
an pan-red bean paste filled pastry
awase zu-seasoned vinegar
azuki-dried red beans

bao-Chinese name for bun
beni shoga-red pickled ginger
bibinka-Filipino coconut rice dessert

char siu-Chinese sweet roasted pork
chow mein-fried noodles
chung choi-salted turnip
cilantro-Chinese parsley, coriander
coconut milk-juice from meat of coconut

daikon-white radish
dashi-soup stock
dashi konbu-dried seaweed (kelp) used for soup stock
dashi-no-moto-Japanese instant soup stock granules
dau see-fermented salted black soybeans

ebi-shrimp

five spice powder-blend of Chinese star anise, cloves, fennel,
          peppercorns and cinnamon
furikake nori-Japanese seasoned seaweed mix

gobo-burdock root
goma-sesame seeds
guacamole-Mexican avocado dip
guava-thin-skinned fruit with slightly acid pulp
gyoza-Japanese dumplings filled with meat and vegetables
gyoza wrappers-thin circles of dough used in the preparation
    of gyoza
hasu-lotus root; also known as renkon
haupia-Hawaiian coconut pudding
Hawaiian red pepper-small, hot, red chili pepper
Hawaiian salt-coarse sea salt
hijiki-type of seaweed
hoi sin-Chinese spicy bean sauce
hondashi-fish-flavored soup granules
horenso-Japanese name for spinach
hibachi-charcoal braiser
huli huli-Hawaiian term for cooking over an open fire

imitation crab-crab-flavored fish product
inamona-roasted, pounded and salted kukui nut
inari sushi-sushi in cone-shaped fried tofu
iriko-small dried fish

kabocha-pumpkin
khal bi-Korean barbecued short ribs
kaki mochi-Japanese rice crackers
kamaboko-steamed fish cake
kanpyo-dried gourd strips
kanten-agar agar
katakuriko-potato starch
kikurage-fungus
kim chee-hot, spicy, Korean preserved vegetable
kinako-soy bean flour
kinpira-stir-fry seasoned with soy sauce and sugar
kiri konbu-finely cut seaweed
ko choo jung-Korean red pepper sauce
konbu-dried seaweed

konnyaku-tuber root flour cake
koshian-strained red bean paste
kumu-Hawaiian name for goatfish

larp cheong/lup cheong-Chinese sweet pork sausage
laulau-Steamed bundle of meat in ti leaves
lavosh-Armenian flat bread
li hing mui-Chinese dried salted plum
limu-seaweed
limu koku-variety of seaweed
lomi-Hawaiian term meaning to crush ingredients with fingers
long rice-translucent mung bean noodles
look fun-wide sheets of Chinese noodles
lumpia-Filipino spring roll filled with meat, vegetables or fruit

mahimahi-dolfin
mai fun-Chinese rice noodles
makina-celery cabbage; won bok
malasadas-Portuguese yeast donuts
manju-bean paste-filled bun
mirin-sweet Japanese rice wine
miso-fermented Japanese soybean paste
mochi-glutinous Japanese rice cake
mochi rice-sweet or glutinous rice
mochiko-glutinous rice flour
MSG-monosodium glutamate
mun doo (man doo)-Korean meat and vegetable dumplings

nachos-tortilla chips and cheese Mexican appetizer
namasu-Japanese vinegar flavored vegetable dish
namul-Korean salad
nasubi-eggplant
nishime-cooked vegetable dish
nishime konbu-narrow kelp used in Nishime
nori-dried purple seaweed sheets; also known as laver

ogo-Japanese term for seaweed
okara-bean curd residue
opakapaka-pink snapper
opihi-shellfish; baby abalone
oyster sauce-Chinese oyster flavored sauce

pansit-Filipino noodle dish
panko-flour meal for breading
passion fruit-fruit with seedy pulp; also known as lilikoi
pipikaula-Hawaiian dried beef; jerky
poi-mashed taro; Hawaiian staple
poke-Hawaiian seafood appetizer
pot stickers-Chinese pan-fried meat and vegetable
        dumplings

saimin-Island term for thin wheat or egg noodles
sake-Japanese rice wine
sake kasu-rice wine residue
sanbaizuke-pickled vegetables in soy sauce, sugar and
        vinegar
senbei-Japanese wafers
sengiri daikon-dehydrated radish strips
shiitake-dried mushrooms
shiofuki konbu-salted, partially dried kelp
shira ae- food combined with mashed tofu sauce
shirataki-tuber root noodle
shiso-beef steak plant
shoyu-Japanese name for soy sauce
shumai/siu mai-Chinese steamed meat dumplings
soba-buckwheat noodles
somen-fine wheat flour noodles
su-Japanese term for vinegar
sumiso-vinegar-miso sauce
suribachi-serrated bowl used for grinding
sushi-Japanese vinegar flavored rice
sushi meshi-prepared sushi rice

taegu-Korean style spiced codfish
takenoko-bamboo shoots
takuwan-pickled turnips
tako-octopus
tamagoyaki-thinly fried egg sheet
taro-tuberous root of taro plant
tempura-fritters
teriyaki-soy flavored sauce
ti leaf-broad leaf of ti plant (Cordyline termenalis) used in
        cooking
tofu-Japanese name for soybean curd
tortilla-Mexican flat bread made of cornmeal or wheat flour
tosa-zu-seasoned vinegar sauce
tsubushian-Japanese unstrained red bean paste

udon-flat Japanese noodles
umani-vegetable-meat dish
unagi-eel
un choi-swamp cabbage

wakame-long, curling strands of seaweed
warabi-fern shoot
wasabi-Japanese name for horseradish
water chestnut-bulb of an Asian marsh plant
won bok-celery cabbage; makina
wun tun/won ton-Chinese dumplings
wun tun pi-thin squares of dough used to wrap meat in wun
        tun preparation; won ton wrappers

yaki manju-baked pastry with azuki filling
yaki niku-Japanese term for grilled meat
yakitori-Japanese style grilled or broiled chicken
yatsumi zuke-relish dish
yokan-sweet azuki bean confection

HEALTHY DIET GUIDELINES

1. EAT A VARIETY OF FOODS

          Fruits and Vegetables
          Whole grain and enriched breads, cereals and grain products
          Milk, cheese and yogurt
          Meats, poultry, fish and eggs
          Legumes (dried peas and beans)

2. MAINTAIN AN IDEAL WEIGHT

          Obesity is a risk factor for many diseases including heart disease, high blood pressure, diabetes, and some cancers.

3. AVOID EXCESSIVE FAT, SATURATED FAT AND CHOLESTEROL

          Choose lean meat, fish, poultry, dry beans and peas as your protein sources.
          Moderate use of eggs and organ meats.
          Limit intake of butter, cream, hydrogenated margarine, shortenings and coconuts oil and foods made from such products.
          Trim excess fat off meats.
          Bake, broil or boil rather than fry.
          Read labels carefully to determine amount and types of fat in foods.

4. EAT FOODS WITH ADEQUATE STARCH AND FIBER

          Eat foods with adequate fiber to reduce cholesterol and glucose absorption in the gastrointestinal system-fiber also reduces risk of diverticulosis symptoms and risk of colon and rectal cancer.

5. AVOID EXCESSIVE SUGAR

          A diet high in sugar promotes tooth decay. Sugary foods are also often high in fat and calories and low in vitamins and minerals.
          Use less of all sugars and eat less of foods containing sugars-i.e.candy, soft drinks, cakes, etc.
          Read food labels for sugar content.

6. AVOID EXCESSIVE SALT AND SODIUM

          Too much sodium in the diet may contribute to high blood pressure, especially for people with a family history of high blood pressure. Un treated high blood pressure can lead to heart attacks, strokes and kidney disease.
          Learn to enjoy the natural, unsalted flavors of foods.
          Use only small amounts of salt in cooking or at the table.
          Limit your intake of salty foods - i.e. chips, pickled foods, cured meats, condiments (soy sauce, garlic salt, etc.)

7. AVOID EXCESSIVE ALCOHOL

          Heavy drinking is associated with cancers of the mouth, throat, esophagus and liver. Cancer risk is especially high for heavy drinkers who smoke. Alcohol also reduces fat digestion causing increased amounts of cholesterol and triglycerides in the blood. In addition, alcoholic drinks are high in calories and low in vitamins and minerals.

WEIGHTS & MEASURES

1 pinch = less than 1/8 teaspoon (dry)

1 dash = 3 drops to scant 1/8 teaspoon (liquid)

3 teaspoons =1 tablespoon (dry and liquid)

2 tablespoons =1 fluid ounce (liquid)

4 tablespoons =1/4 cup = 2 fluid ounces (liquid)

5 1/3 tablespoons =1/3 cup (dry and liquid)

8 tablespoons =1/2 cup = 4 ounces (liquid)

12 tablespoons = 3/4 cup = 6 fluid ounces (liquid)

16 tablespoons =1 cup = 1/2 pint = 8 ounces (liquid)

2 cups =16 ounces (liquid) = 1 pint (liquid)

4 cups = 32 ounces (liquid) = 2 pints = 1 quart (liquid)

16 cups =128 ounces (liquid) = 4 quarts = 1 gallon (liquid)

1 tablespoon =15 milliliters

1 cup = 250 milliliters

1.06 quarts =1 liter

1/4 pound =125 grams

1/2 pound = 250 grams

3/4 pound = 375 grams

1 pound = 500 grams

SUBSTITUTION OF INGREDIENTS

For	Substitute
1 tablespoon flour (as thickener)	1/2 tablespoon cornstarch, potato starch, rice starch or arrowroot starch or 1 tablespoon quick-cooking tapioca
1 cup sifted all-purpose flour	1 cup unsifted all-purpose flour minus 2 tablespoons
1 cup sifted cake flour	7/8 cup sifted all-purpose flour, or 1 cup minus 2 tablespoons sifted all-purpose flour
1 cup corn syrup	1 cup sugar plus 1/4 cup liquid*
1 cup honey	1 1/4 cups sugar plus 1/4 cup liquid*
1 ounce chocolate	3 tablespoons cocoa plus 1 tablespoon fat
1 cup butter	1 cup margarine, or 7/8 to 1 cup hydrogenated fat plus 1/2 tea spoon salt, or 7/8 cup lard plus 1/2 teaspoon salt
1 cup coffee cream (20 percent)	3 tablespoons butter plus about 7/8 cup milk
1 cup heavy cream (40 percent)	1/3 cup butter plus about 3/4 cup milk
1 cup whole milk	1 cup reconstituted nonfat dry milk plus 2 1/2 teaspoons butter or margarine, or 1/2 cup evaporated milk plus 1/2 cup water, or 1/4 cup sifted dry whole milk powder plus 7/8 cup water

1 cup buttermilk or sour milk	1 tablespoon vinegar or lemon juice plus enough sweet milk to make 1 cup (let stand 5 minutes), or 1 3/4 teaspoons cream of tartar plus 1 cup sweet milk
1 teaspoon baking powder	1/4 teaspoon baking soda plus 5/6 teaspoon cream of tartar, or 1/4 teaspoon baking soda plus 1/2 cup fully soured milk, or buttermilk, or 1/4 teaspoon baking soda plus 1/2 tablespoon vinegar or lemon juice used with sweet milk to make 1/2 cup or 1/4 teaspoon baking soda plus 1/4 to 1/2 cup molasses
1 tablespoon active dry yeast	1 package active dry yeast or 1 compressed yeast cake
1 whole egg	2 egg yolks or 3 tablespoons plus 1 teaspoon thawed frozen egg, or 2 tablespoons and 2 tea spoons dry whole egg powder plus an equal amount of water
1 egg yolk	3 1/2 teaspoons thawed frozen egg yolk, or 2 tablespoons dry egg yolk plus 2 teaspoons water
1 egg white	2 tablespoons thawed frozen egg white, or 2 teaspoons dry egg white plus 2 tablespoons water

* Use whatever liquid is called for in the recipe.

Notes

INDEX OF RECIPES

PUPUS & BEVERAGES

BREADS, RICE & NOODLES

MAIN DISHES

Poultry

SOUPS, STEWS & SALADS

Soups & Stews

SWEETS

VEGETABLES

ETC., ETC., ETC.

PART IV
OUR FRIENDS & SUPPORTERS

Did You Know Pohaku Ki'i or Petroglyphs Were Visible in Mo'ili'ili?

In the 1930s archaeologists discovered two groups of pohaku ki'i or petroglyphs in the Mo'ili'ili district on the north bank of Palolo Stream, about 400 feet east of the Saint Louis Street bridge. The petroglyphs were about 25 yards apart, but the figures were so indistinct that they could hardly be seen even within a few feet. In one group, there were eight human figures which were all solid. The other group of pohaku ki'i consisted of five solid figures. Although the archaeologists decided that these stone carvings were done hastily without much care, they agreed that they were old and "certainly the real thing."

Glen Grant

Notes

ACKNOWLEDGMENTS

The Moiliili Community Center and its Cookbook Committee extend a special "mahalo" to each of the following Hawaii businesses and organizations, MCC members, Moiliili residents and friends for their generous donations and contributions to this book. This cookbook represents the culmination of countless individual efforts. We apologize for the inadvertent omission of any names.

Aloha Poi Bowl   Carol's Bake Shop   Koraku Restaurant
Maple Garden   Nuimono-Hawaii   The Willows
Original Waioli Tea Room

Rebecca Ryan, MCC Executive Director
Donna Y. Shiraki Hashimoto, MCC Board of Directors President
Mrs. Robert (Alice) Masuda

Senator and Mrs. Daniel Inouye   Governor Benjamin Cayetano
Lieutenant Governor Mazie Hirono   Senator Matt Matsunaga
Senator Brian Taniguchi   Representative Scott Saiki
Representative Terry Nui Yoshinaga

Former Governor and Mrs. George Ariyoshi
Former Mayor and Mrs. Frank Fasi
Mrs. Helene Matsunaga

Laura Arakaki   Sharlene Arita   Leatrice Chee
Randy Chee   Raelene Chock   Elizabeth Clark
Elaine Costello   Tamiko Fukumoto   Grace Furugen
Alice Goss   Rose Hiranaga   Nobuye Horio
Robert Hsu   Amy E. Ibaraki   Bessie Imata
Yaeko Inouye   Muriel Kaneda   Faithye Kaneshiro
Zana W. Luis   Charles Mason   Carol Matsukawa
Shizuko Mukaida   Eleanor Nonaka   Jean Okamura
Jane Otsuka   Stella Saito   Dee Sakamoto
Judith Saranchock   Carol Shiraki   S. Stewart
Alice Takahashi   Dorothy Takizawa   Doris Toda
Florence Tokuda   Catherine Tomita   Nancy Tsuda
Lorraine Tsuneda   Sarie Uechi   Sue Wada
Jennie Wong   Heidi Yamamoto   Rachel Yorita
Lue Zimmelman   Laurie Wong   Becky Covert
Celeste Imamura   Lynn Kazama   Patsy Kirio
Teri Kondo   Laura Mau   Cyndi Osajima
Sue Saiki

And the many donors who contributed recipes anonymously

227

Notes